Ghosts of Central Arizona

Heather Woodward

Photography by Stacy Fortson

Foreword by Mark Boccuzzi

Schiffer Publishing Ltd®
4880 Lower Valley Road, Atglen, Pennsylvania 19310

Other Schiffer Books on Related Subjects:

Scare-Izona: A Guide to Arizona's Legendary Haunts
978-0-7643-2844-2, $14.95

Tucson's Most Haunted
978-0-7643-3153-4, $14.99

A Journey through Northern Arizona
978-0-7643-3010-0, $24.99

A Journey through Southern Arizona
978-0-7643-3269-2, $24.99

Ouija is a registered trademark of Parker Brothers Games.

Library of Congress Control Number: 2009932170

Designed by Stephanie Daugherty
Type set in GreckoDeko/NewsGoth BT
ISBN: 978-0-7643-3387-3
Printed in China

Schiffer Books are available at special discounts for bulk purchases for sales promotions or premiums. Special editions, including personalized covers, corporate imprints, and excerpts can be created in large quantities for special needs. For more information contact the publisher:

Published by Schiffer Publishing Ltd.
4880 Lower Valley Road
Atglen, PA 19310
Phone: (610) 593-1777; Fax: (610) 593-2002
E-mail: Info@schifferbooks.com

For the largest selection of fine reference books on this and related subjects, please visit our web site at:

www.schifferbooks.com

We are always looking for people to write books on new and related subjects. If you have an idea for a book please contact us at the above address.

This book may be purchased from the publisher.
Include $5.00 for shipping.
Please try your bookstore first.
You may write for a free catalog.

In Europe, Schiffer books are distributed by
Bushwood Books
6 Marksbury Ave.
Kew Gardens
Surrey TW9 4JF England
Phone: 44 (0) 20 8392 8585; Fax: 44 (0) 20 8392 9876
E-mail: info@bushwoodbooks.co.uk
Website: www.bushwoodbooks.co.uk

DEDICATION

☠ To Dave Flores, who "invested in my future" and gave me the financial support to write this book.

☠ To my son, Tyler, who is my anchor and the center of my Universe.

Acknowledgments

Rudy Cortese: Let's not have pie together, okay?

Gail Cortese: Thanks for being a great travel guide.

Mom, Dad, and Lisa: Thank you for being my biggest supporters.

Dave (my step-dad): "Ooga Booga with Heather!"

Cassidy, Donovan, and Ophena: Never settle for anything less than your dreams.

Nate, Rachel, Sarah, and Cassandra: Blood is always thicker. Thanks for your love and support.

Katie: Thank you for editing.

Mark B.: Thank you for writing the foreword and the Starbucks banter.

Marla Brooks: The catalyst for synchronicity.

Debbie Altherr: Thank you for taking the time to tell me the ghost stories of Jerome.

Stacy: Thank you for taking pictures at the last minute.

Chad Saunders: Thank you for the years of friendship and the thankless hours of listening to me implode.

Z: You always seem to be there for those pivotal points in my life, and you have always forced me to write from the heart.

CONTENTS

Contents

Foreword:

A Scientist's Perspective

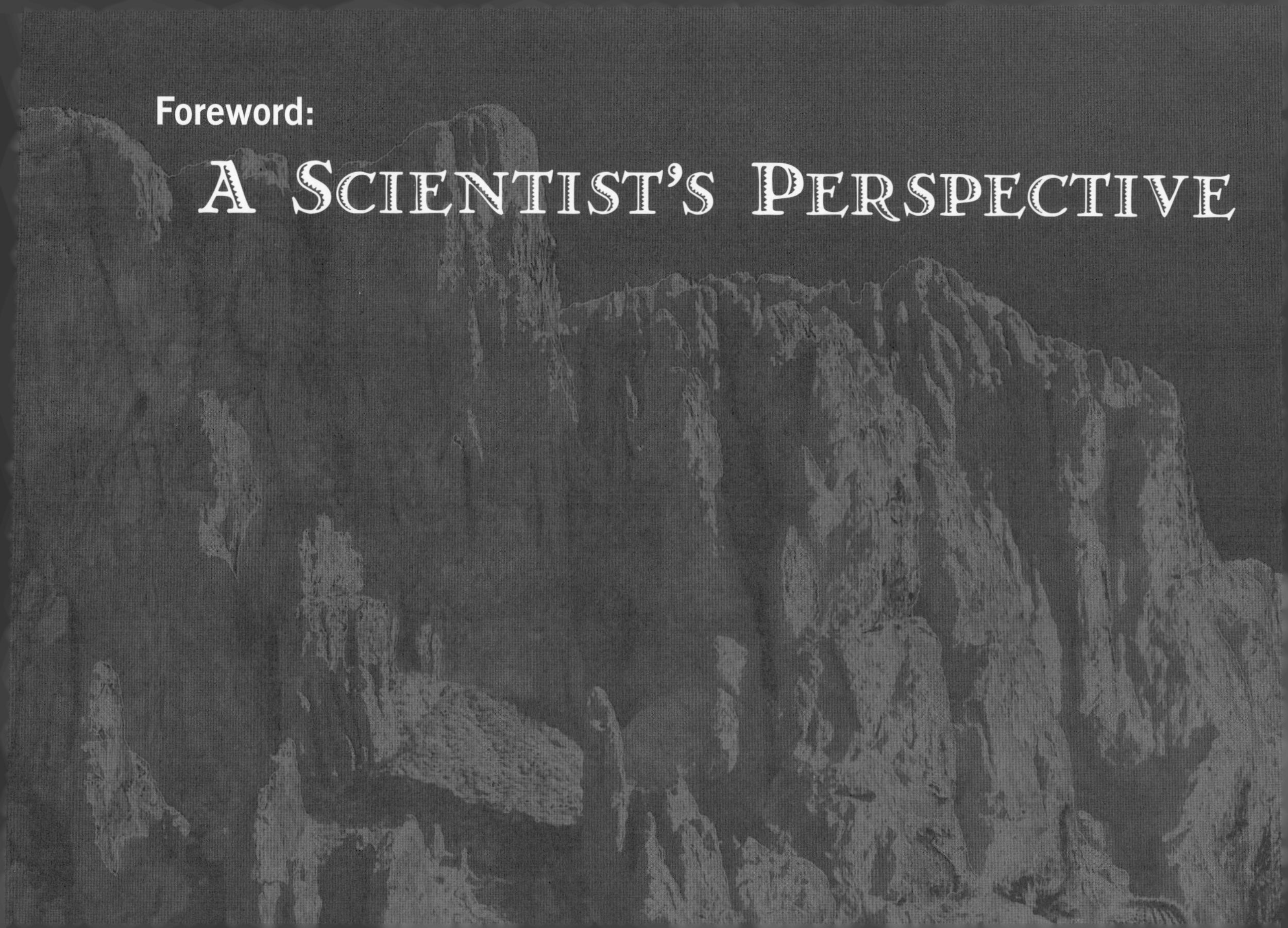

FOREWORD

The Importance of Investigating Ghosts and Hauntings

When we talk about investigating reports of ghosts and hauntings, we are really talking about researching the idea that some aspect of the human personality survives physical death. In parapsychology, this is known as the Survival Hypothesis or simply as Survival. Researchers define Survival as the continued existence, separate from the body, of an individual's consciousness, personality, identity, or self after physical death.

As a Survival Researcher, I'm often asked why the study of Survival is important. While ultimately we all know what happens after we die—having insight about the existence of an afterlife may have important benefits for the living—my research centers on applying what we learn through Survival research to health care, specifically hospice care, grief counseling, and recovery. In addition, the findings from this research may provide allopathic physicians with an alternative view of death. This would allow them to focus on a patient's quality of life rather than simply prolonging life. For these and other reasons, I consider Survival research to be a critical area of inquiry.

When talking about the study of Survival, it is helpful to think of it as a platform that is constructed out of a number of different planks. Each plank is an area of research that produces evidence for a phenomenon that is supportive of the Survival hypothesis. We say "supportive" because it is actually very difficult, at this point, to prove Survival. To understand why it is so hard, we need to talk a little bit about consciousness. Obviously, an in-depth discussion of consciousness is far outside the scope of this introduction, but it is important to touch on it just to demonstrate some of the problems that need to be considered when talking about Survival.

Consciousness seems to be the current buzzword. Everyone is talking about it, but what is it? That's the problem. We really don't know what consciousness is, how it works, or where it resides. Find this hard to believe? Then try this: Prove to me that you exist. Since I can only perceive you through my own consciousness, there is no way that you can prove to me that you are real and not simply in my mind. ("I think, therefore you are.") Really. No argument will hold up. I can't even prove to myself that I'm real. And even if we concede that we both exist, where does consciousness happen?

Researchers in this field fall (roughly) into two broad camps: 1) consciousness is produced by and resides in our brains (people who share this view are called materialists); and 2) consciousness resides outside of our bodies and our brains, allowing it to manifest locally with our bodies; that is, the brain is a receiver of a non-local consciousness (people who hold this view are called dualists).

So, if we can't prove how and where consciousness exists while we are alive, how can we prove that it exists/continues after we die? This brings us back to the Survival platform. Each area of research, or plank, provides some compelling evidence that is supportive of Survival. However, taken on its own, each plank cannot prove the existence of an afterlife.

To illustrate this idea, imagine a single wooden board, a plank if you will, that is bridging two blocks. It is wobbly and unstable and if you stand in the center and bounce around, it just might break. Now, by adding more planks, side-by-side, and securing them together, you get a stronger platform that can support you. This is the same for Survival. Taking into account the combined research from a variety of different areas, the support for Survival becomes more solid.

While some researchers and authors may omit some of these areas or include others, below are what I consider to be the major planks in the Survival platform (listed alphabetically): Apparitions of the Dead and Hauntings, Mediumship, Near Death Experiences (NDEs), Out-of-Body Experiences (OBEs), Reincarnation, Technology-Enhanced Discarnate Communication and Interaction (TEDCI)

While much of the research into these areas is conducted under highly controlled conditions in the laboratory, much of the investigation into Apparitions of the Dead and Hauntings can really only be done in the field. From a scientist's perspective, this kind of field research is by far the most challenging. It is time-consuming, expensive, and often does not produce conclusive results.

In addition, proper controlling for confounding variables in field research can be difficult.

This is where paranormal investigators like Heather come in.

Paranormal investigators who utilize careful methodologies and publish their findings (like the ones read about in this book) play a critical role in helping scientists understand the nature of the haunting phenomena being reported by people all over the world. By searching out allegedly haunted locations and documenting their own experiences during investigations, Heather and other paranormal investigators provide important information for scientists like me. Their work forms the development of controlled field and laboratory experiments that may ultimately provide greater support for Survival.

It is through this collaboration between paranormal investigators and scientists that we may be able to finally answer the question humans have been asking since the beginning of our existence: What happens to us when we die?

Mark Boccuzzi
Survival Researcher,
Windbridge Institute for Applied Research in Human Potential
www.Windbridge.org
www.FindingGhosts.com

Introduction:

The Paranormal Beginning

Introduction

The idea of ghosts and the afterlife have been around for as long as there have been humans wandering Earth. Most cultures have incorporated some sort of afterlife into their belief systems, mostly through the implantation of superstitions and mythology. Usually, ghosts were something to be feared — a representation of the cursed or the damned. Even today, in the Japanese culture, spirits are the stuff made of horror films, hence the crop of ghost-based tales like, "The Grudge," "The Ring," and "Shutter." It seems more than ever we are equally frightened and intrigued by the supernatural.

This intrigue has fueled a whole subculture of TV shows, reality or otherwise, where ghosts are the center characters. In these shows, there are two types of investigators: the technical-based teams and the psychic-based teams.

The technical-based shows use equipment and logic to tackle paranormal issues, bypassing the idea of personal experience or intuition and how it plays into paranormal phenomenon. Their objective is to document paranormal activity, reveal it to their clients, and move on to the next case. There is very little in dealing with the psychological impact of the haunting or easing their client's anxieties. Either the location is haunted or it isn't... based on data collected from their technical equipment. End of story.

Psychic-based shows are more sensational, but they focus on the human experience and the psychological aspects of the paranormal (mostly fear-based). The prime objective of psychic-based shows is to identify what is causing the paranormal activity and ease the client by getting rid of the paranormal phenomenon.

It seems that the clients on these shows are plagued by negative paranormal "beings" like demons, possessed dolls, aggressive entities, and the type of paranormal phenomenon that, even though they exist, are rare in nature. It's ludicrous to think that a team of psychic-based investigators can waltz in, armed with a banishing spell, and rid a ghost or negative entity in one fell swoop. There are certain mechanics to a haunting that are too complicated for such a simple remedy. Most paranormal issues are based on the intricate aspects of human relationships, whether those involved are dead are not. There are ways to deal with a haunted situation to ease those involved especially those neutral parties whose only crime was to live in a house where a traumatic event occurred. They may include banishing rituals or pagan themes if that is the religion of the persons involved; but banishing a ghost from a location is not usually the most effective way to control a haunting (and it rarely works). Nor is it representational of what happens in a typical paranormal case. Furthermore, it is based on a false premise that a ghost can be easily dismissed by the cadence of a mystical incantation. Sorry, life isn't a Joss Whedon supernatural drama.

While I love these shows and readily watch them, you must remember that television is for entertainment purposes only. Usually, paranormal shows are shot over a three-day investigation period and then slickly edited down into forty-five minutes of exciting footage enhanced by creepy music, quick shots, and eerie special effects. What you see on television is not really how an investigation works. A TV show is a business managed by a stressed producer who has invested a large chunk of cash into the program, the success of which is reliant on viewers and produced in such a way to keep viewers wanting more. Don't expect your personal paranormal excursions to be anything like those you see on TV, that is, unless you travel with an orchestra, a set of producers vying for ratings, a full camera crew, and a sound guy.

Comparing television paranormal investigating to real paranormal investigating is like comparing a carrot to a Big Mac. Both have elements of nutrition, but the Big Mac has hip packaging that makes it seem bigger and cooler. However, the carrot, with its simple orange exterior and thin build, has the powerful surge of beta carotene and vitamin A that makes it a much more worthy competitor. The carrot would win against the Big Mac in a UFC steel cage match, hands down.

TV paranormal shows are Big Macs. The paranormal investigating you will be doing from this book is the carrot. It is a simple approach based on a fusion of the technical and psychic techniques of ghost hunting. Although the technical and the psychic approach seem mutually exclusive, they are really two sides of the same coin. This method of investigating bridges the technical tools of ghost hunting with other divinatory tools that help you trust your intuition and further your personal experiences. Also, it can give you a heads-up (through your intuitive abilities) so that you can anticipate paranormal activity a few seconds before it happens.

Most of the stories and experiences written here have been culled through more than one personal experience or my own paranormal experiences while performing psychic-based investigations. Still, that does not guarantee when you go to these places, the activity will be thriving. There are so many factors that go into experiencing activity it's a wonder that we experience anything at all. There will be long hours where nothing happens. It will be only you sitting in the dark fantasizing about how you could be playing Guitar Hero instead of staring blankly at a wall wishing something would finally happen. However, when you finally hear that knock, or you see an apparition floating down the hall, or the door slams in front of you, those are the golden moments that you will never forget. Those are the moments that will reshape your thinking and force you to contemplate those bigger questions that don't have answers (yet).

Are there really ghosts? Is there life after death? Where do I go when I die? With each experience, hopefully, you will come closer to finding your own answers to these questions. When you are in the trenches, investigating on your own terms, there will be rewards that last longer than forty-five minutes with commercial breaks. The process will take longer, and you won't get immediate results; but when you do get results they will be profound. You will have an appreciation for life that will last...well, a lifetime.

What's Next?

Now that you have learned more than you ever wanted to know about the technical and psychic aspects of paranormal investigating, the next step is to buy the appropriate equipment based on your objective and level of experience. If you are just starting out, the basics will suffice, and later you can decide whether the technical side, the psychic side, or both are the best approach.

If you're going to be strictly a technical investigator, then focus on putting together a strong kit that you can rely on to give you accurate results, gleaning information from various technical and experimental tools. For those of you who want to rely on your intuition and work with your own energy, don't buy anything at all. Practice developing your sixth sense; buy a book on psychic development or simply go in cold and see what you come up with. If you're going to go the route sans equipment, I suggest bringing some paper and a pencil to write down your impressions. Or bring an audio recorder specifically for expressing psychic impressions. This way, later, you can fact check them against actual history.

If you're going the psychic route and don't want to rely only on your intuition, make a pair of dowsing rods or buy a pendulum. Practice with them to see how they resonate with your own energy. You may want to try spirit communication with an Ouija Board, an Ovilus, or a Ghost Box to see what kind of results you glean.

You may even find that you don't need the tools. You may become an "accidental" medium.

For those who want to incorporate both the technical and psychic aspects of ghost hunting, all of the above applies. Just make sure that there's a good balance between the technical and psychic equipment — and don't forget to put down the gadgets and trust your intuition.

When I am investigating with my paranormal group, Paranormal Investigators of Southern Arizona (P.I.S.A.), we use a strict protocol that combines the technical and psychic approach. Our methodology incorporates a set of checks and balances, so that our psychics and mediums are always being counter-checked by our technical investigators. Impressions are never considered evidence unless they are researched and found to be credible by a historical reference. Anomalous readings are scrutinized against base readings, personal experiences, and psychic impressions. Our investigations are videotaped, audio recorded, and catalogued through digital cameras. Everything is put together and whatever can be disproved or cannot be referenced is thrown away. Whatever is left over is questioned until it's finally considered paranormal. It's a long and tedious process, but it garners substantial quality results. We get very little EVPs, hardly any photos, and only a handful of video anomalies, but what we have we stand by because it has gone through some rigorous testing.

You don't have to be as die-hard as P.I.S.A. Paranormal. We use our strict protocol to help private residents and business owners with paranormal issues, so our findings have to be air tight and our methodology reflects that.

Whether you are an armchair investigator going on vacation to look for a thrill or a serious investigator searching for answers into the unknown, make sure you know your equipment, your intent for investigating, and treat your surroundings and your spirit friends with the utmost respect. If need be, create your own protocol or methodology that represents your objective and follow through with it. Or throw caution to the wind and just start investigating. Whatever you decide, be practical and logical about your findings. Don't be afraid to question, scrutinize, and debunk. You'll get better results that way.

How to Use This Book

This book is a compendium of haunted locations in the Sedona, Jerome, Flagstaff, and surrounding areas. Each location has a history rich with the will and intrigue of the human spirit, which provides the basis for paranormal activity. Use the history and activity reported as guide to what sort of paranormal activity you may expect at each location. If you're working with intuition or psychic tools, forego reading the history and ghost stories until after your investigation. This way you can use it as reference to substantiate your findings.

In certain locations, I have provided my own psychic impressions and personal experiences. Some matched up with paranormal phenomena already reported. Other experiences were purely my own. If you have a paranormal or psychic experience, own it, even if it doesn't match up with anything reported in this book. Just because it hasn't been written down doesn't mean that someone else hasn't had the same experience. Not every paranormal story is recorded. Certain people like to keep their paranormal experiences to themselves due to fear of the unknown or of being ridiculed.

Paranormal activity seems to be more prominent in some locations and less so in others. The reason for this is unclear, but all hauntings are not created equal. Always go into a haunted location ready for the big phenomenon to happen, but expect nothing to manifest. Never let your guard down completely, and stay focused. Activity is rarely reliable and the littlest thing can trigger paranormal activity.

Each location has directions or an address for easy routing, hours of operation if applicable, and a phone number for rates, reservations, and other inquiries. Most locations are open to paranormal investigating. Many of the managers and staff will even share their ghost stories or provide additional history if you inquire, so be personable and don't be afraid to ask questions. More than not you will get positive results.

However, to be on the safe side, I advise calling ahead to see what each location's policies regarding paranormal investigating are at the time. I have found that certain locations can be fickle depending on how much exposure or notoriety they are receiving from their ghostly inhabitants. Sometimes management changes or businesses are sold or the location decides to go in another direction that does not cater to the paranormal world. Just because at one time a location was open to paranormal investigating does not mean they are right now. Everyone is entitled to change their minds.

The Mythology of Ghost Stories

Mostly, ghosts are born from a rich history, which fuels their existence and forces them in a holding pattern, repeating the past over and over without recourse or resolution. Whether it's the sudden release of emotion from a murder or the constant frenetic energy of a brothel, there is a long list of theories as to how heightened situations create an environment that nurtures paranormal activity. How those environments produce a placed memory apparition or an intelligent ghost are still being questioned and scrutinized. In the meantime, we're left with a minefield of theorized explanations that hinge on the speculation that there is life after death and that ghosts are an integral part of the cycle of spiritual evolution. In all cases there is only one point that has been established; paranormal activity, in its many conceptions, requires the human experience.

A placed memory apparition is much easier to comprehend because it is essentially a tape recording of an incident trapped in a loop of time. The apparition has no consciousness and repeats its fate without cognitive patterns. Even though it can be unnerving to experience a placed memory apparition, there aren't any moral dilemmas attached to them.

Intelligent specters are more daunting to contemplate because they display thoughts and emotional traits established by the living. They react and communicate in a way that is familiar to us, even though for all intents and purposes, they aren't supposed to be here on the earthly plane. It begs explanations to theological or philosophical questions that don't yet have answers.

What can be established are the similar stories that you will encounter in your ghost-hunting travels. There are the stories of the lady donning a white dress, levitating down hallways of hotels; the disembodied clanking sound of cowboy boots adorned with spurs in saloons; the French perfume lady whose lavender or lilac scent lingers down hallways or at the foot of stairways, though no one is there. There are also the sounds of parties in empty lobbies, the smell of cigar smoke in no-smoking areas, and the sound of children laughing in quiet hallways. You will notice that no matter where you travel, there will be similar paranormal phenomena with familiar ghost stories. You can count on being told a story of a "lady in white" in every old hotel — it's just part of the mythology of paranormal investigating.

It doesn't make it any less fascinating, though. These similarities will fuel your curiosity, compelling you to contemplate what all the "ladies in white" have in common. What about their personalities kept them from crossing over? Why are they seen more than other apparitions? Why are they always seen in white?

Most people who have had an unexpected encounter with the paranormal are eager to share their stories. Even if it is similar to tons you have heard before, the experience has profoundly impacted the storyteller, furthering their human experience; perhaps, furthering their cycle of spiritual evolution in some small way. So, even though we do not know why or how the "lady in white" still creeps down hallways in her billowing period dress, her memory lives on with each person who sees her. And, hopefully, her life was not in vain ... if she is able to move us forward with understanding in our own lives.

Section One:
Paranormal Investigating

We have all seen the television shows or movies where a group of technical paranormal investigators approach a client's house in their flashy black van, with big bold letters etched on the side, stating their exact purpose: GHOST BUSTERS. As the team struts up to the door, sporting garish t-shirts with their group's logo prominently displayed across their chests, everyone in the neighborhood knows that you have a paranormal problem. While the team unpacks their menagerie of high-tech gadgets from the van — spools of wire, the quad DVR system, an external audio system, a thermal imaging camera, laptops, and monitors — into the home, the neighbors are calling each other and the looky-loos have congregated on the corner to find out what kind of craziness is happening on their street.

The fact is, there is still a stigma about paranormal activity and the average client prefers discretion and anonymity to a big black van announcing its intention, parked in front of their house, making them the topic of conversation at the next neighborhood picnic. Although, all the high-tech equipment looks cool, most of the time, it can be excessive and it can cause undue stress by making a spectacle of an already sensitive situation.

Discretion is even more important when investigating in public locations like restaurants and hotels. Although most haunted locations thrive on the business from curious investigators, there are those patrons who aren't keen on the idea of co-habiting in the same space as a ghost. Those who are interested will ask and maybe meet an investigation buddy, but for the most part, the "don't ask, don't tell" rule applies to paranormal investigating. So, leave the black van at home.

The basic tools of ghost hunting will fit discreetly in a backpack or a utility vest and will be less conspicuous. That will give you more time to investigate rather than having to explain why you are monkeying around with a quad-camera infrared surveillance system that you have hooked up in hopes of catching the full-body-apparition you read about in this book on film.

You will get more funny looks than ones of piqued interest. Keep your odd hobby to yourself and don't cause attention unless you want to risk not being able to come back to what could be a prime paranormal spot.

1

The Tools

There are two types of tools you can use for paranormal investigating: technical and psychic. Most people are more familiar with the technical tools even though the psychic tools have been around longer and were the staple for spirit communication and paranormal investigating before the age of technology. Still, for some reason, there is a misconception that if you don't have some sort of battery-operated gadget in your hand, then you aren't effectively investigating. Nothing can be further from the truth. Most times your body will sense paranormal activity way before your gadget does. There will be an anticipatory feeling fluttering in your stomach right before something anomalous happens.

Pay attention to your own body's senses: did the room suddenly get colder or darker? Are you feeling unnaturally nervous or tense? Are you feeling nauseated? Are you short of breath or dizzy? Did the room get eerily quiet? These are all telltale signs that paranormal activity may be brewing. If you can learn how to use your own senses (including your sixth sense, we all have one) in conjunction with technical gadgetry, you will have a more rounded paranormal experience.

Technical Tools

Really, the only tool you need for paranormal investigating is yourself. However, a good personal experience doesn't seem to hold credence anymore in this day and age of technology. People want to see some sort of tangible result from their efforts; something they can share with other people.

Before making the commitment to buy a ton of equipment, first, figure out what your objective is for ghost hunting. Is it a hobby or an obsession? What do you hope to prove? Are you searching for the answers to those large questions or are you in it for the thrill? Do you want to investigate by yourself or do you want to start a group? How much time do you have to dedicate to investigating? What is your budget?

If you take the time to answer some of these questions and be practical about your motives and your budget, then you will have a better idea of what kind of equipment is essential and what can be put on a wish list. No matter if you have time to spare and a have huge cash flow, there are some basic pieces of equipment you should acquire. Some pieces you may already have, other pieces are relatively cheap and should be affordable for any budget.

Electromagnetic Field (EMF) Detectors

The Electromagnetic Field Detector is probably the most commonly known tool for paranormal investigating. It's also the least understood. The popular misconception is that an EMF detector can "detect" ghosts, but really it should be used to gauge environmental electromagnetic fluctuations to determine the by-product of paranormal activity. Meaning, the detector will not lead you to a pocket of paranormal activity, but it will give you an indication of activity that is happening or has happened.

Originally, EMF detectors were designed to locate man-made electromagnetic fields that are caused by electricity. While natural electromagnetic fields tend to stay static, man-made fields fluctuate constantly as the current runs through the electrical wiring. The electromagnetic field can be constant whether the source (e.g. kitchen appliance) is on or off, but it's usually more prominent when the source is on. Common sources for electromagnetic fields are computers, televisions, electrical outlets, and kitchen appliances. Also, walkie-talkies and cell phones produce a large electromagnetic field when in use.

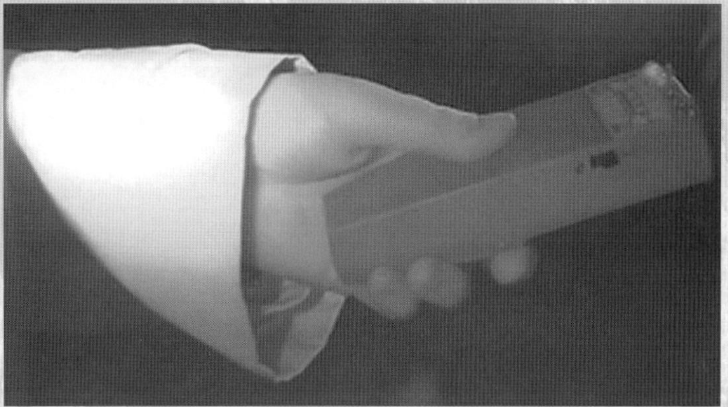

A KII Electromagnetic Field Detector.

Although there is no scientific evidence that EMF detectors are useful for paranormal investigating, the common theory suggests that a paranormal presence may disrupt an electromagnetic field by using it as an energy source to communicate. This disturbance creates a surge in the electromagnetic field, which creates a spike in the fluctuation and then quickly dissipates back to normal. The short burst gives the ghost its own electromagnetic field for a few short seconds, giving it enough energy to show its presence. Your EMF detector will read the short spike as a by-product of the activity.

Typically, EMF-based paranormal activity will happen in a short burst and then just as quickly fade away. Constant fluctuations, no matter how unusual, are not usually associated with paranormal activity. If you search hard enough, you will probably find the culprit. Beware of any external sources including radio towers, airports in the vicinity, and old piping. Metal can be an impressive conductor and carry an electromagnetic field throughout the entire location, creating all kinds of "anomalous" readings.

EMF detectors measure electromagnetic fields in milligauss. A typical reading should be between 1-10 milliguass. Nearly all appliances and gadgets will fall under this reading. Even humans give off a small amount of EMF, between 1-3 milliguass. Anything above 10 milligauss is considered a high reading and could be a point of interest for paranormal activity.

A theory, based on the work of Dr. Michael Persinger, suggests high electromagnetic fields may be the cause of paranormal phenomenon usually associated with a haunting. Dr. Persinger compared thirty-seven years of documented hauntings in *Fate Magazine* to geometric activity that happened on the same dates of the reported paranormal activity. He found a distinct correlation between geometric activity and paranormal activity, which inspired him to research high electromagnetic fields on the human brain.

Dr. Persinger experimented with high electromagnetic energy on the temporal lobe to find out if his subjects experienced any of the paranormal attributes associated with a haunting. He found that most did experience anxiety, feeling a presence or someone watching them, seeing dark shadows, and hearing unexplained noises; all of which are common in most paranormal cases.

Yet, another theory states that high electromagnetic fields stimulate dormant parts of our brain, thereby causing a gateway between dimensions or alternate realities. This merging of realities allows the brain to interpret what normally cannot be seen...the results being the paranormal phenomenon associated with a haunting.

In either case, there is strong correlation between paranormal activity and high electromagnetic fields, whether the activity is a dimensional merging or a figment of the imagination. One thing is for certain—in areas where the most paranormal activity is reported, there will be strong electromagnetic field readings, especially in hotels and other structures with more than one floor. Usually, the ceiling lighting from the first floor will directly affect the EMF readings on the second floor, where most of the paranormal activity will be reported. Going with that premise, the basement, where electrical boxes are stored, have high incidents of paranormal activity, as well.

It is essential to understand how electromagnetic fields work in order to properly investigate a location. Most EMF detectors function in the same way. However, take the time to figure out the pros and cons of your instrument before using it in an investigation. As tedious as it may sound, reading the manual will give you all kinds of pertinent information that will give you an edge on a paranormal investigation.

Using an Electromagnetic Field Detector

There is a correct way and a wrong way to handle an Electromagnetic Field Detector in an investigation. Celebrity investigators on television do NOT handle their EMF detectors correctly. Waving your instrument in the air will not give you an accurate reading because electromagnetic fields are not constant and fluctuate rapidly. If you're reading an increase in your electromagnetic field while waving around the EMF detector, you are merely picking up on the high curve of its natural fluctuation. No matter how cool it looks, it's *not* paranormal. It's just plain inaccurate.

The best way to get an accurate reading requires little movement. Hold your EMF detector at about an arm's length from your body. Or if that's uncomfortable tuck your elbows in for support. Take a couple of steps, wait for the detector to stabilize, and then take note of the reading. Walk another few steps and repeat the process. If you need to take a reading above or below you, slowly move toward the area and wait. Don't take the reading until the meter is static in your hands and the reading stabilizes.

EMF detectors should be used for two separate functions while paranormal investigating: to calculate base readings and for spirit communication.

An EMF detector should be used to sweep the environment for electromagnetic fields and to calculate the base readings. These base readings will give you an indication of how strong and wide the electromagnetic fields are in an environment and how they will affect your investigation.

Also, note how large of an electromagnetic field your other equipment produces and take heed before packing your environment with gadgets. Make sure you know how your equipment affects your environment and what their base readings are alone and used together. Without knowing your equipment readings, you run the risk of false positives.

Video cameras and all battery-operated gadgets, especially cell phones, GPS, and walkie-talkies, will render some sort of electromagnetic field. Even other people or investigators can affect the reading of an EMF detector, especially if everyone is gathered around the gadget in a tight circle. Also don't forget that infrared heat registers an electromagnetic field. So, the more infrared-based equipment you have, the more you are affecting your environment.

EMF detectors can be used for spirit communication. The premise of spirit communication via EMF detectors suggests that a ghost can interact with the instrument by manipulating the electromagnetic field around it, thereby causing a noticeable spike. This spike is read differently depending on which EMF detector you own. On needle-based detectors like the Gaussmaster or Trifield Meter, the spike will show as the needle ascends rapidly for a split second and then descends to the base reading of the environment. Needle-based EMF meters have a built-in alarm that can be turned on for low-light use. The alarm will go off, indicating a rapid change in the fluctuation of the electromagnetic field.

Other meters are equipped with lights and are more convenient for spirit communication because the paranormal presence may be able to manipulate the lights in a pattern. For instance, with a cell sensor, you can ask the presence to blink the red light once for "yes" and twice for "no."

KII Electromagnetic Field Detector

The KII Meter is the most commonly used EMF detector for spirit communication because the meter has five-colored LED lights ranging 1-5 milligauss all the way up to 20+ milligauss. The circular lights are easy to read in the dark and they give more range than a cell sensor-style EMF detector which only blinks red if it registers near or above 5 milligauss (in its default setting.)

KII meters have only been introduced to paranormal investigating in the past few years, and there is still a lot of controversy as to why or if the meter is effective in spirit communication. The controversy looms around whether or not to hold the KII meter in your hand or to set it down.

The detector has a lever in the middle of its body that you push down with your thumb to turn it on. One school of thought suggests that you must hold the KII meter in your hand, pressing the lever firmly down with your thumb in order to use it for spirit communication. The ghost will interact with the device by using your own body's electromagnetic field to assist in answering questions. It does this by causing slight nervous tics in your arm, which in return force your thumb to react in the correct manner to communicate the spirit's intent.

Another camp-of-thought suggests there are too many unconscious factors in play when holding the KII meter in your hand. A hand-held device has a high risk of subtle manipulation whether or not the holder is aware of his unconscious intentions. Therefore, a penny should be slipped into the lever forcing the KII into the "on" position. Then the KII should be placed on a flat surface for easy viewing. This way if there is a positive result to a question, there is no doubt that it is paranormal in nature.

Even so, there is no real definitive proof that spirits can communicate through EMF. While an anomalous "answer" to a spoken question is exciting and coincidental, there is no real way to gauge whether or not it's paranormal given that EMFs are constantly fluctuating. Most questions seem to be asked randomly, but really, we are creatures of patterns. Usually, we pause in between questions about the same amount of time. If there is an undetected fluctuating electromagnetic field in the environment, the high point of the current could sync with the pattern of your seemingly random questioning, thereby mimicking positive spirit communication. The point being, take time to really get to know your environment and make sure you understand how the workings of the electromagnetic fields in the area. That way if there is indeed paranormal activity, there will be no question of its authenticity.

Flashlights

Although not for the fashion conscious, a head flashlight is the most convenient for paranormal investigating because it will free up your hands for other equipment. When buying a head flashlight, make sure that it comes with a red gel setting. When investigating in the dark, a bright light will mess up your night vision and it's obnoxious to other investigators. The red gel setting will filter the light enough to be able to see what's in front of you, but won't be glaring.

If you opt to buy a hand-held flashlight instead, make sure that it's lightweight and durable. Most new flashlights come with blue, red, and green gels. If they don't, spend the extra few bucks to buy a gel pack kit. Gel pack kits are great for older flashlights if you have one lying around that you want to use for ghost hunting. Gels come in almost every size to accommodate any flashlight. To add to your flashlight, usually it's just a matter of unscrewing the rim of the flashlight and laying the gel on top of the light.

Batteries

Almost every piece of equipment you get will require batteries. Buy them in bulk in every size and store them in your freezer. Make sure to pack extra batteries in your ghost hunting kit. Batteries have a tendency to drain quickly in haunted locations.

Thermometers

Thermometers are another piece of paranormal equipment used incorrectly based on lack of knowledge and misconception. A lot of ghost-hunters are excited to acquire one, but then rarely take it out of their kit because it doesn't render assumed results. Mostly this happens because the paranormal investigator did not take the time to properly learn how to use it.

There are two types of thermometers: surface and ambient. Surface or contact thermometers should primarily be used for base readings and to find the flow of air currents caused by air conditioning and heating systems. Contrary to popular use, surface thermometers will not work to find cold spots. Surface thermometers will only read the temperature emitted from the point of the contact, not the temperature of the air. If there is an air current in the path of the point of contact, the temperature reading will be an average of the surface and the air system the infrared beam has passed through. This is helpful when trying to map how currents flow in a structure. However, it will not give you any indication of cold spots. It will only tell if there is an unnoticed air current that is cooling down the location, thereby negating a paranormal response.

Contact thermometers are most effective in buildings or other structures. They aren't accurate outside because of wind and other environmental factors. To use the thermometer in a structure, the thermometer should be pointed at the surface. The infrared beam shoots out of the point of the thermometer when the finger tripper is depressed. The red laser you see is not the infrared beam; it's a visual guide for the user to gauge direct the point of contact. The invisible infrared beam hits the surface and the thermometer calculates the temperature of that surface only. Every surface should have its own reading. Base readings are calculated by taking an average of all the surfaces in the room.

Ambient thermometers measure direct air temperature. For this reason they are best for finding cold spots. Most ambient thermometers have a probe for inserting into the alleged cold spot. You can remove the probe and take the temperature of the air to compare readings. Make sure to re-calculate surface temperatures as well, just in case a cold air current isn't the culprit for the alleged cold spot.

Ideally, you should acquire a surface thermometer and an ambient thermometer. You will be able to get your base readings with the surface thermometer, finding drafts and air systems and charting how they flow. Then, with the ambient thermometer, measure the room temperature. With both calculations, you will be able to better assess whether a cold spot is true or just an air current flowing through the room.

Video Cameras

Video cameras are still pricey if you are on a budget. However, they are a great investment if you're able to purchase one. When buying a video camera make sure that it has true infrared or "night shot" capabilities. Some of the less expensive video cameras are not truly infrared. The "night" feature opens the shutter letting in more light, which will give your recordings a streaky quality that is hard to watch. True infrared will actually highlight the area you are recording even in pitch black. If you can afford it, an external infrared light source is a valuable asset for your video camera. It will broaden your range of viewing and make your tape clearer.

Cameras

Digital cameras are the cheapest and easiest way to take pictures for paranormal investigating. They have a USB output to dump pictures easily onto your computer and they are relatively inexpensive. The only drawback from digital camera is that the shortness of their lenses can cause more orb photographs than a more costly 35 mm camera. Still, if you are aware of your surroundings, knowing that a dusty or humid area will probably be a rich ground for picking up orbs, you can easily distinguish what should be considered paranormal and what should not.

Heather Woodward, P.I.S.A. Paranormal investigator, using a Sony video camera with Night Shot and an attached external infrared light.

Use a digital camera to document the layout of your environment in case there are areas of concern later. Make sure to snap panoramic views of the location to be thorough. Always snap more than one angle of the same area. That way if there is an anomaly in a picture, you have other views to work with for debunking purposes. If you can, take off the camera strap on your camera so that it won't accidentally get into your shot. Straps show up in pictures as white and streaky anomalies and can be mistaken for an apparition. Also, keep your fingers away from the lens. Fingers are often mistaken for anomalies too.

Try and keep your pictures as basic as possible. Don't use any fancy settings or the black and white functions. Complicated settings alter the picture and it's an added layer of processing that isn't needed. If you catch an apparition or anomaly, you want it to be clear and distinguishable and without any question of what it's supposed to represent.

There are now free programs online that read the metadata on digital pictures. The metadata will tell you the type of camera the picture was taken from, which settings on the camera were used, and if it was altered in graphic software like Photoshop. This is a great way to make sure that any pictures you are shown are legitimate. If you're going to be showing your pictures to the public, be are aware that metadata software is easily accessible and the cleaner your pictures, the less they will be scrutinized.

Audio Recorders

Audio recorders are used for spirit communication to try and capture electronic voice phenomenon (EVP). Most ghost hunters use digital audio recorders because they are lightweight, compact, and you can store more than one track on them. The newer digital audio recorders have a USB output, which makes for easy downloading straight to your computer. With headphones, you can listen to the track in an audio-editing software program and cut audio clips as you go along. If you don't have audio-editing software on your computer, check the Internet. There are many that you can download for free that are simple and easy to use. Digital audio recorder capture is the simplest and convenient method for recording electric voice phenomenon.

However, there are those who believe that the compression of digital audio recorders taints the audio, especially after being manipulated in a computer, which is another layer of processing. For this reason, many paranormal investigators still use old-fashioned analog tape recorders for their EVP work.

Theory suggests the electromagnetic qualities of the analog tape recorder aid in spirit communication. The tape recorder uses its electromagnetic field to turn the tape into a magnet that helps the voice of the spirit "stick" to the audio recording. Supposedly, analog-taped EVPs are more frequent and clearer because there are no compression or binary conversion issues that you have with audio digital recordings. If you want to try the analog tape method but don't want to lug around an old cumbersome tape recorder, there are many smaller compact dictation tape recorders on the market that use mini-tapes.

In either case, whether you decide to go for the convenience of a digital recorder or you want to experiment with analog tape, an external microphone is essential. An external microphone will keep you from recording the whirring sound audio recorders make, especially analog tape recorders which have an internal motor. Also, a microphone will give you a louder recorder with a longer range.

Additional Equipment

If you have an ample budget, there are a plethora of gadgets you can buy for paranormal investigating, but they aren't necessary. Mostly, they are less practical and are good for additional experimenting and research above and beyond typical ghost hunting.

Thermal Imaging Cameras

A thermal imaging camera is probably the most coveted piece of equipment by the average paranormal investigator. However, very few ghost hunters ever get their hands on one because of its exorbitant price. Most likely, you have seen investigators on TV walking around with one, searching for unseen apparitions and cold spots. However, the likelihood of something anomalous appearing on a thermal imaging camera is about the same as with any other less-expensive video camera. It just looks cooler.

Contrary to popular belief, a thermal imaging camera does not register heat. It works just like a regular video camera, but instead of recording visible light, the camera shows mid-and-far infrared. Surfaces in direct contact of the camera will emit (rather than reflect) mid-and-far infrared, giving off a temperature that reads as color.

Perhaps a ghost that is invisible to the naked eye may be able to emit a temperature reading, but since there is no substantiated evidence that a ghost is made of matter, it's hard to hypothesize whether or not a thermal imaging camera would be able to pick up an apparition.

Like a contact thermometer, a thermal imaging camera reads surfaces, not ambient air temperature. For this reason, it's not the best alternative for finding cold spots. Instead of showing the cold spot, it may find the surfaces in the area that are cold and could accommodate for the sudden drop in temperature. While it's good information to have, it's more practical to purchase a good video camera with "night shot" and surface thermometer. Save the extra money rather than purchase a redundant piece of equipment.

Ion Detectors

Air ion counters detect natural and artificial positive and negative ions. Natural ions include those generated by radon gas, fires, evaporating water, and lightening storms. Before a storm, positive ions increase, while during a storm negative ions increase. Artificial sources are ion generators (like home air filter systems,) improperly grounded air conditioning systems, combustion vapor, and electrically charged or heated surfaces. Most any high-charged or electrical incident will create some sort of change in the rate of ions in the air. Using the premise that ghosts use electromagnetic fields in short bursts for communication, then it would affect positive and negative ions or ionize the environment.

The air ion counter is used to track the by-product of a ghost or the ionization of the high-charged burst of energy. However, ion counters are expensive, fussy gadgets that are not straightforward and have a low percentage of accuracy (about 25%). There are many natural contributing factors that will set off the detector including something as simple as static electricity or a brewing storm. Also, fires highly affect the air and will produce a higher reading of negative ions. So, a significant reading can't be totally ruled out as paranormal. There are other pieces of equipment, like an EMF detector, that can be used for by-product ghost detection that are less expensive, more stable, and more accurate.

Geiger Counters

Geiger counters detect microwave radiation. Primarily, they are used to measure radon in the environment. Theory suggests that ghosts produce some sort of radiation when they manifest, which a Geiger counter can detect. The theory is highly speculative, and a Geiger counter is not worth its hefty price tag (cheap ones start around $400) unless you are going to be doing some intense scientific research on the subject. The average ghost hunter should just stick to the basics.

Experimental Equipment

In the last few years there has been an upsurge of new experimental equipment in the paranormal field. These new gadgets are mostly innovative ways to collect electronic voice phenomenon and further spirit communication.

Ghost Boxes

Ghost boxes are a fairly new concept in the paranormal field. The idea of communicating to the dead through a two-way communication device may have started with Thomas Edison. Though rumors circulate, there is no evidence to substantiate the claim.

In 1979, George Meek and Bill O'Neil created "Spiricom" (short for spirit communication), a device comprised of 13-ton generators that spanned the range of the adult male voice. As a person spoke into the Spiricom, his voice got "wrapped up into the buzzing noises" of the generator asking a spirit to communicate. The different frequencies were supposed to be a carrier for any disembodied voices that wished to come through, using the tones of the human voice.

Eventually, Meeks and O'Neil began to get results with the Spiricom. They claimed that the voice of Dr. George Jeffries Mueller, a NASA scientist and personal friend communicated through the machine in twenty conversations over the span of three years. Dr. Mueller even gave Meeks and O'Neil advice on how to improve the Spiricom. Although, the Spiricom gleaned positive results, the experiment has never been successfully recreated. Still, the Spiricom was the pioneer in the concept of ghost boxes and the idea of two-way, real-time spirit communication.

In 2002, Frank Sumption created "Frank's Box," a box using white noise and an AM receiver to communicate with spirits in real-time. Sumption got the idea for his experiments using the computer software, EVP Maker, created by Stefan Bion. Frank's Box consists of a white noise generator fed through a random volt generator. The random voltage is linked to an AM radio, which forces the receiver to turn to a specific spot on the radio dial changing every split second.

The premise of the communication is that the spirit can interact with the changing AM radio dial to "speak" through the device. The newer versions of Frank's Box use a "sweep method." The AM band tunes back and forth, creating snippets of broadcasting stations, which the spirit can manipulate into phrases or sentences. Sumption has made over twenty-five boxes to date and has published his schematics on the Internet so others could create their own.

Recently, a ghost box has been created called, the "Radio Shack Hack," which is a modification of a Radio Shack radio. Essentially, you take apart the radio, clipping the "mute" function so that the radio freely sweeps across the AM/FM band mimicking the "sweep method" of the new Frank's Box. Many paranormal investigators use the Radio Shack Hack because the radio is easily accessible, cheap (about $25), and the modifications are simple. There are "how to" videos online that are simple to follow. It's much easier make a Radio Shack Hack than to figure out the schematics for a complicated Frank's Box when, relatively, they do the same thing.

Ovilus

The Ovilus is a small, lightweight gadget created by Bill Chappel, a retired electronics engineer, for "environmental communication." The device works by measuring fluctuations in the "environmental" energy fields and turning them into audible speech using a synthesizer chip, an English word dictionary, and a function that sounds out words phonetically. The Ovilus is powered by a 9-volt battery and has two audio-out jacks so that you can use headphones and an external audio source simultaneously. It has small red LED lights for use in the dark.

The Ovilus has seven modes of operation: The first is a dictionary speech mode that will pick up words from the more than 512-word dictionary; the second uses Phonemes, the individual sounds that make up speech, to phonetically sound-out energy changes; the third mode mixes both the dictionary and the phonetic modes to give a wider range of sounds; and the fourth mode gauges electromagnetic field values. The fifth mode says "yes" or "no" by calculating the average of fluctuations in the energy field. If the fluctuation is twenty-five percent higher than the last reading, the Ovilus will say "yes" and, if it's twenty-five percent lower, then it will say "no." The sixth mode only shows energy levels through the LED lights. Finally, the seventh mode uses the pattern of the LED lights to act as a digital dowsing rod. For instance, if the lights on the left side stay on, it means to turn left, and if all the lights go on to the right and left, then it means to go straight.

The Paranormal Puck

Another invention by Bill Chappel, the Paranormal Puck is a small, square, black box that hooks up to a Windows based computer through a USB port. There are nine sensors on the puck that gauge A and B voltage, electromagnetic fields (two sensors), natural electromagnetic fields (four sensors), and temperature. The puck can be used for two separate functions: raw data collection and spirit communication. For raw data use, the Paranormal Puck logs and time-stamps the raw environmental data from its sensors onto the computer for later use. Or you can watch the data in real time to establish patterns of fluctuation in the environment.

In "environmental communication mode" (ECM), the raw environmental data is modulated into allophones, phonetically sounding out speech from its 2,000-word dictionary. If you're performing an EVP session and asking questions with the Paranormal Puck in ECM mode, the spirit may be able to cause fluctuations in the environment to create the proper phonetic response.

Divinatory Psychic Tools

Though not as widely known as the technical tools, divinatory or psychic tools have been around for centuries, aiding in fortune telling and spirit communication. Using divinatory equipment in conjunction with technical equipment will give your investigation a good balance. You should not wholly rely on gadgets, but on your instincts as well. Divinatory tools will help in trusting your intuition.You will be surprised at how your technical equipment and your divinatory equipment will come up with the same positive results.

Dowsing Rods

Dowsing rods are the oldest tool for divination and are still used to locate water. Other uses for dowsing rods are locating unmarked graves, determining the sex of an unborn child, and ghost-hunting. There are two types of dowsing rods: Y-shaped and L-shaped. Generally, the L-shaped dowsing rods are used for paranormal investigating. Dowsing rods are usually made from brass or another lightweight material. You can even make your own by unfastening two wire coat hangers and bending them into an L-shape.

To use dowsing rods, hold the shortest parts in your hand letting the longer pieces point outward. Wait a few moments to get a feel for how easily the rods swing back and forth. They should be able to cross over each other with ease. However, at the start point, they should be held stationary, parallel to each other. It may take a few tries before you can steady them in your hands.

There are two ways you can use the dowsing rods. Ask "yes" or "no" questions, using the open position as one answer and the crossed as the other answer, or you can concentrate on finding anomalous energy, cold spots, or any other area that may have paranormal activity. The rods should point to the direction that you need to go. When you come to the location with activity, the rods should cross.

Pendulums

A pendulum is a rounded object with a point at the end that is hung by a chain or cord. Usually, they are made of crystal, semi-precious stone, or metal. You hold the chain in-between two fingers, holding your elbow with your other hand for leverage. Try to keep as steady as possible so that you are not influencing the pendulum with your slight movements. As soon as you can keep the pendulum from moving, ask if a spirit would like to communicate with you. The pendulum should start to move in a back-and-forth or circular pattern. Ask the spirit to reverse the pattern, and wait to see if it does. After you have determined that the pendulum will swing in both directions, assign one way for "yes" and the other way for "no," and begin to ask questions.

If you want to ask more complex or detailed questions, there are pendulum boards and books you can buy that have the alphabet, numbers, and/or phrases on them. Or you can cut out a paper circle to make your own board with answers to specific questions you would like to ask. Just hang the pendulum over the board, making sure to keep your arm steady. Ask a question and wait for the pendulum to swing to the appropriate response.

Intuition

Yes, your intuition is a tool. It is probably the most important tool in paranormal investigating. Pay attention to your body's natural responses in an allegedly haunted environment. It is the single best tool to gauge paranormal activity. All hauntings are based around the human experience, and what better way to gauge paranormal activity than your actual, human body?

Are you getting dizzy? Are you nauseated? Are you feeling watched? These are all context clues that there may be something paranormal buzzing around you. Vocalize what you are feeling into your audio recorder, no matter how stupid it may seem at the time. Trust yourself and the information you are receiving.

Express any dates or names that flit into your consciousness and make note of uncomfortable areas in your body. They may correlate to real events that happened in the area you are investigating. If you are feeling led in a certain direction, then follow your intuition and go. There's no harm in being wrong, but you will notice that most of the time your reactions will be dead-on and a few seconds ahead of your equipment.

Ouija Boards

Ouija Boards have so many negative superstitions surrounding them that it's hard to believe their earnest beginnings. In the 1880s, during the height of the Spiritualism Movement, anyone who had psychic or medium abilities was in great need, but what about those who didn't have any well-developed intuitive attributes?

The Ouija Board (originally called a Talking Board) was thought up as an alternative to table-tipping and other such techniques used by mediums to speak with the dead. With a Talking Board, *anyone* could practice spirit communication even if they didn't have any natural ability. In 1886, an article in the *Tribune* was printed explaining how to create your own talking board and gliding pointer to communicate with your "spirit friends."

In May 1890, Elijah Bond filed the first patent for the "Ouija Board," sighting Charles W. Kennard and William H. A. Maupin as the assigners. His patent was finally granted almost two years later in February of 1892. Legend states the name "Ouija" came from a series of Talking Board sessions with Kennard. The spirit communicating with Kennard told him to name the board "Ouija" because it was Egyptian for "good luck." Incidentally, "Ouija" is not the Egyptian word for "good luck," still, the name stuck. It is unclear as to why it took so long for someone to mass-produce the Talking Board as a novelty item. However, the Ouija Board or "Egyptian Luck Board" became an instant hit.

Later, William Fuld gained rights to the Ouija Board, and as part of his marketing strategy, revamped the history of the board. He said that he chose the name "Ouija" by merging together the French word "oui," meaning "yes," and the German word "ja," also meaning "yes." This became the first of many mythologies and superstitions about the Ouija Board. Fuld's company made Ouija Boards up until the rights were sold to Parker Brothers in 1966. Presently, they are still the manufacturers of the modern-day Ouija Boards.

Using an Ouija Board

There are two contradictory beliefs about why Ouija boards work: the automatism theory and the spiritualist theory.

The Automatism theory says that through "ideomotor response," or your unconscious, movement forces the planchette into action. Somehow, the Ouija Board creates a shortcut in your brain from the conscious to the

P.I.S.A. Paranormal investigators, Stacy Fortson (right) and Michele Durco (left), use an Ouija Board for spirit communication in a paranormal investigation.

unconscious. The "messages" spelled out on the board are your unconscious thoughts, not spirit communication. When a group of people get together to use the Ouija Board, they are using "Collective Automatism," where all parties are unconsciously linked.

The Spiritualist Theory conveys the idea that the Ouija Board is a conduit for spirit communication. The spirit is able to use the planchette to express their message to the living. Proprietors of this theory believe that ghosts and other ethereal forces are benign and have only positive intentions for communicating with us.

So, why does the Ouija Board get such a bad rap? Many people believe if the Ouija Board can be used as a portal to the "other side," then not only can benign spirits with well-intentioned messages come through, but negative or darker energies can come through as well. Many believe that a negative entity will pretend to be a spirit in order to trick you into believing that you are in contact with a spirit and eventually possess you. The entity does this by reading your mind and conveying personal information to you so that you are put at ease and trust that the entity is there to help you. Eventually, you will become obsessed with the Ouija Board and its personal messages, wanting to play with it alone. Finally, when the entity has you alone, it will force its will on you and inevitably possess you. To protect from this, there are all sorts of superstitious rules about how to use an Ouija Board. The first rule being: never use it alone.

There's no substantial proof that the Ouija Board can cause possession or a myriad of other supernatural maladies. I have worked with Ouija boards and never had anything dark or strange happen to me. However, I have been on more than one paranormal investigation (without equipment) where I have been pushed or had things thrown at me. In either case, being smart and using common sense is necessary.

There is no difference between standing in a dark room with an audio recorder and EMF detector asking a ghost to interact with you or using a planchette and an Ouija Board to ask a ghost to spell out its message. Both situations put you in a precarious position where the outcome is reliant upon forces that we know little about. But, for some reason, technical gadgetry is an accepted method of spirit communication while the Ouija Board will continue to be the redheaded stepchild of the paranormal field.

I say forget about the superstitions and try out an Ouija Board. Make a decision based on experience, logic, and common sense, not years of mystical fabrications produced by pop-culture urban legends. It just may be a new resourceful tool that yields positive results.

2

Types of Hauntings

We don't really know why or how hauntings are created. There are a lot of speculations, but largely, it is agreed that the two most common types of hauntings are the placed memory haunting (also called residual haunting) and intelligent haunting.

Memory Haunting

Placed memory is the most common type of haunting and usually occurs in structures with a rich history that entails a heightened sense of emotion or where a traumatic event has occurred. Theoretically, a placed memory haunting is caused by extreme emotion including lust, anger, stress, or fear. The heightened emotion forces the person's "essence" or "energy" out of the corporeal body so quickly that it leaves an imprint in the actual molecular structure of the location, changing it forever.

There have been instances where a traumatic event caused a house to be haunted. Eventually, the house was torn down and a new structure was built. However, the new structure became haunted even though the new building's history held no traumatic events.

It is believed the structure itself holds the imprint, with the porous, natural building materials soaking in the expelled energy of the traumatic event like a sponge. However, when the building is torn down, the energy stored in the natural materials is released into the "air," changing its molecular structure forever. The area becomes like a tape recording of the event, replaying aspects of it over and over again.

Though the paranormal activity may seem random, in a placed memory haunting there will be some sort of recognizable pattern. However, those who are witnessing the activity may be so distracted by the actual occurrence that they forget to logically break down what is happening so that it makes sense. As the fear becomes heightened, so does the activity. Effectively, the fear of the activity feeds the paranormal incidents, making them more pronounced and the occurrences more frequent. This is usually when a paranormal investigator or a psychic is called in to find out what is really happening. With a little bit of knowledge and logic, the activity can be toned down. It will never go away, but if a pattern can be established, then the fear is diminished. With an established pattern, there can be comfort. Most people can live with what is expected. It's the randomness that can't be explained that breeds fear and unwittingly strengthens the activity.

Some signs of a placed memory haunting are cold spots, a lingering displaced feeling, disembodied footsteps, voices, or unusual repetitive sounds. You may encounter an apparition, but it will not interact with you. Instead, it will repeat an action or show up in the same location like a looped video. Sometimes, doors and windows will open and close, but it will be because of energy expansions, usually caused by stress from the living inhabitants adding to the trapped energy in the location.

Intelligent Haunting

Intelligent hauntings are what is typically considered to be a ghost. These types of hauntings have been immortalized in horror movies, making them seem like an everyday occurrence, when really, they're are not at all commonplace.

Ghosts are considered "intelligent" because they will interact with the living inhabitants of the structure. Usually, they will have some sort of emotional attachment to the location, stemming from an emotional or traumatic event. Other times the ghost will have unfinished business that keeps them from leaving this world. In all cases, it seems to be a personal decision for the ghost *not* to move on to the other side, which makes it that much harder to get them to leave the location.

Intelligent hauntings can be very frightening, especially since most of the time the ghost is trying desperately to interact with you, which means the activity may be frequent, intense, and seem personal. In movies, this sort of activity is shown as negative, evil, or destructive giving it a negative stigma and adding to the fear factor of an intelligent haunting. In reality, you must remember (usually) the ghost is not trying to hurt you, but trying to get your attention.

However, personality consciousness is thought to carry over in an intelligent haunting. So, if the person was a grumpy, negative person in life, then he will undoubtedly be a grumpy, negative ghost. That doesn't mean there is harmful intent in the haunting; it just means that you may not be dealing with a very happy person. Also, most ghosts don't cross over because of something traumatic that happened to them, which means, emotionally, they are stuck in a dysfunctional problem that needs to be remedied. You may feel their frustration or negative emotions and preconceive that as evil, when really, you are experiencing normal base emotions.

Some signs of an intelligent haunting are slamming doors or windows, moving objects, practical items going missing and then found in an unusual location, faucets, lights, and electrical appliances flickering on and off, disembodied voices (usually personal, like whispering your name), a cold wind or chill, and the strong feeling of a presence. Sometimes you will see the apparition in full form as they looked before they died.

Poltergeists

We have all seen the movie, but most don't know the characteristics of a true poltergeist haunting. At first poltergeists were thought to be mischievous ghosts wreaking havoc: throwing objects, moving furniture, turning lights on and off, knocking on walls, and in some more extreme cases, causing fires. Now, it is believed that the source of the phenomenon is a "human agent" or someone living in the environment that has strong psychokinesis and a reservoir of unexpressed emotions or sexual tension. Usually, the activity revolves around one person in the household — commonly a pubescent or teenage girl — and when the person leaves, the activity ceases.

The poltergeist phenomenon increases exponentially during stressful times and subside during happier moments. Mostly, the activity will materialize around household objects or other personal artifacts in the house, and sometimes target one person in the household, if the "human agent" has unresolved issues surrounding that person.

Orbs

Orbs are the most controversial topic in the paranormal field. Bring up orbs and you are sure to start a heated debate. Are they proof of the paranormal or are they refracted dust? As long as there are orb pictures, there will be speculation. However, there have been many skeptical paranormal researchers who have successfully reproduced orbs under controlled conditions that look exactly like those pictures that claim to be paranormal. In the Webster dictionary "paranormal" is defined as "not scientifically explained." Therefore, if the average paranormal investigator can deliberately replicate an orb in a picture, then by its very definition an orb cannot be considered paranormal in nature.

Still, an "orb-a-phile" will defend the honor of his or her orb pictures to the bitter end. Usually, they will explain that there were balls of light that were seen with the naked eye that illuminated from out-of-nowhere and then disappeared just as suddenly. Sometimes they slowly streak across the sky. Other times they hover in midair. There is no explanation for this sort of phenomenon and therefore orbs are considered paranormal.

While the reports of these kinds of orbs *are* unexplainable, they are somewhat rare and pictures of them are hard to come by. The popular belief is that these sorts of orbs are not ghosts, but balls of excess concentrated energy from the Earth. While they look cool, they may not be of paranormal nature.

Others believe the anomalous lights are the beginning of a spirit. The photographer catches the burst of energy caused by the spirit before it forms into a full-body specter. Why there is no picture of the actual apparition is questionable. How does a photograph pick up the burst of orb energy, but not the apparition itself?

The other point an "orb-a-phile" will argue is that they felt the "presence" of a spirit right before they took the picture and that is when they caught the orb. Personal experience should never be discounted, and it is a highly intriguing claim. Was there a ghost standing in the very spot when the picture was taken?

Although this picture is creepy, it has no paranormal attributes. The orbs are from dust and moisture in the air.

Why did it not show up in the picture? We will never know until humans become more evolved or someone creates a technology that will be able to undoubtedly track ghostly activity. In the interim, there are many speculations as to why the presence is felt and only an orb remains—or rather a refracted dust particle.

The common explanation suggests the spirit (unseen by the naked eye) stirred up the air in the spot where it was standing. So, you cannot see the apparition, only its effect on the environment. Still, at the end of the day, a refracted piece of dust will remain a refracted piece of dust, and though personal experience has its own merits, it cannot be considered true evidence unless it's backed up by something tangible. Unfortunately, if you pull out your orb explaining — it's the stirred up air of an apparition that didn't show up in the picture — it might not go over so well.

Whether you believe in these claims or not, the average orb photo can be easily explained away and debunked as dust or moisture. It's better to deal with other types of "evidence" that are less controversial and have some merit in the paranormal field. However, if you want to fight the good fight in the name of "orb-a-philes" everywhere, then snap those pictures and display them proudly. However, be prepared to be on the receiving end of some heated criticism.

Electric Voice Phenomenon (EVP)

The Electric Voice Phenomenon is the most popular "evidence" of paranormal activity next to personal experience. However, a personal experience is speculative based on your own memory of the incident and does not hold any tangible attributes. Pictures are subjective due to the many factors that can alter them including weather, dust, operator error, and graphic software manipulation. Video still holds merit, but it's rare that something authentic is ever captured that cannot be explained. Although EVP has its own set of issues, it is more widely accepted as paranormal activity because it is less likely to be explained or tampered with.

The Electric Voice Phenomenon is voices (and sometimes sounds) detected on audio recordings that weren't heard at the time of the recording. Usually the voice directly answers a question or comment relevant to the topic of the audio, and the length of the answer is a few short words. Rarely, are EVPs full sentences. If the voice is audible during a spirit communication session, whether or not it is directly answering questions or interacting, it is considered a disembodied voice, not an EVP. The nature of an EVP is that it can *only* be heard through playback at a later time.

Electric Voice Phenomenon can be heard on an audio track forward or backward. This is another reason why many investigators still use analog tape. Although, most editing software will reverse an audio track, it's much more convenient to manually manipulate it. The only drawback is that in order to isolate the clip, you will have to record it to another external source, such as your computer or a digital audio recorder, which negates the purpose of recording analog in the first place.

Like most everything in the paranormal field, there are many theories as to why electronic voice phenomenon happens, the most popular being that the spirit interacts with the electromagnetic energy of the electrical device to effectively communicate. Another theory states spirits vibrate on a higher frequency and audible communication by a spirit cannot be heard by the human ear. The audio recorder will pick up all sounds no matter the range and compress it into something audible for the human ear. An example of this theory would be the sound of a dog whistle. If you blow on it, you won't be able to hear the sound it makes. However, if you were to record someone blowing on a dog whistle, the sound of it would be on your audio track during playback.

Another, more skeptical theory, suggests electric voice phenomenon is not spirit communication, but the unconscious thoughts of the questionnaire being imprinted in the audio through psychokinesis. This would account for the many EVPs that state phrases like, "Get out!" or "Help!" They can be indicative of the paranormal investigator's instinctual fear from the stress of being in an allegedly haunted environment. Others speculate that the imprints of unconscious thoughts are really the spirit using the questionnaire's electromagnetic impulses to communicate. The reason being, the spirit was once housed by a corporeal body and now knows how manipulate the body's own electromagnetic field to imprint messages onto the audio recorder.

A Brief History of the EVP

EVPs are a relatively new concept in the paranormal field. Spirit communication became popular in the late 1800s because of the Spiritualist Movement. Mediums were used to conduct séances and table-tipping sessions where the spirit, channeled through the medium, answered questions through a series of knocking or sometimes disembodied voices.

Not until the late 1920s were the first speculations of ghost communication via technology ever discussed. Some attribute Thomas Edison as being the first person to consider building a device that could be a telephone to the dead. He even spoke about it to a reporter for a *Scientific American* interview. Later, Edison was cited as denouncing the idea as a hoax and that a spirit communication machine was never in the works.

In 1936, Attila von Szalay started recording electric voice phenomenon on his phonograph records. Later, in the 1950s, his findings with his partner, Raymond Bayless, were published in the *American Society for Psychical Research*. However, the first EVPs to be made public were not until 1959 and were by Friedrich Jürgenson. His recordings of bird songs contained messages from what seemed to be a human voice. Later, the messages became personal and were thought to be from his dead mother.

Still, EVPs were not introduced to the English language until 1971, when Colin Smythe, an avid researcher of electric voice phenomenon, published

Breakthrough, a book by Konstantin Raudive Ph.D., who was a student of Jürgenson and took his work further. Raudive used the phrase "Raudives Voices" to describe human voices he recorded because there wasn't a phrase invented to accurately describe the phenomenon. Colin Smythe coined the phrase "electronic voice phenomena," which is now widely accepted as the standard language.

Capturing EVPs on Tape

It is important to establish a protocol for EVP sessions that will take account of any extraneous noises and keep them from becoming false positives. The single most common error when recording electric voice phenomenon is not accounting for background noise. When in the midst of an EVP session, noises such as cars, other people, pets, and coolant systems are easily identifiable, but if not catalogued, will be harder to distinguish during playback.

Conducting an EVP Session

- Make sure everyone is either sitting or in a comfortable position so there is minimal movement from the participants;
- Place a camera on a tripod in a corner or somewhere in the environment where it will videotape a panoramic view of the electric voice phenomenon session. Later, if you have any questionable background sound, you can refer to the video and try to locate the source;
- Turn on the recorder and state the time and date of the EVP session. Have everyone participating in the session say their name into the recorder. This will help match up voice tonal qualities if there are any questionable phrases or sentences during playback;
- Place the EMF detector on a flat surface or the floor in plain view of all the participants and the camera. Also, you can add a KII or another EMF detector if you wish to ask the spirit to interact with it;
- Ask questions in thirty to sixty second intervals. Refrain from asking "yes" or "no" questions unless you are trying to get the spirit to communicate through the EMF detector and catch its response on audio as well. Speak loudly and clearly, making sure not to whisper. If someone moves, coughs or

their stomach growls, or if there is any obvious background noise, announce it to the room. Or arm one person with a log sheet, a watch and a pen with the sole purpose of cataloguing every extraneous sound.

- Sessions should be between fifteen and thirty minutes long. At the end of the session, thank the spirit for communicating with you. Make sure that all videotape and/or log sheets are labeled with the appropriate location and put in a safe place;

- When listening for electric voice phenomenon, wear headphones. If you suspect a clip of audio is an EVP, send it to at least two other people; preferably, one person who went on the investigation to see if they recognize any familiar sounds on the recording and one person who did not go on the investigation, to verify what you are hearing is an anomaly. If you have them, check your video and/or log sheets to make sure the sound cannot be reconciled.

Classifications of EVPs

Sarah Estep, founder of the AA-EVP, is attributed as being the inventor of the EVP classification that is widely used today. However, Konstantin Raudive used a similar system in his book, *Breakthrough*. Although, we do not know who exactly invented the classification, it is used as the standard for electronic voice phenomenon playback.

- **Class C** – The voice has a faint or whispery quality and its meaning cannot be deciphered. The EVP can only be heard with headphones, but does have paranormal qualities such as a voice that sounds mechanical.

- **Class B** – The voice is distinct and the meaning can be deciphered, although may not be agreed upon. The voice can be heard without headphones, although the meaning may not be distinct enough to be heard without them.

- **Class A** – The voice is clear, distinct, and loud, and the meaning is indisputable. The EVP and its meaning can be heard without headphones.

Section Two:

SEDONA

Often called "Red Rock Country," Sedona is an upscale retirement community with a population of around 11,000 residents. The city thrives on its tourism capital hosting between 1-2 million tourists a years. It is located at the lower end of Oak Creek Canyon and surrounded by the Coconino National Forest. Known for its red rock formations, Sedona is said to glow a brilliant red-orange when the sun rises or sets. The gorgeous landscape has been the backdrop for many western movies including "Broken Arrow" with James Stewart.

Indians were the first to inhabit the area that is now Sedona. They were a tribe of nomadic hunters and gatherers finally settling in the Verde Valley. Between 900-1350 AD, the Sinagua, a more civilized tribe of Indians, settled in the mountains, building pueblos and cliff houses. The Sinagua were knowledgeable in farming and were able to cultivate gardens of vegetables in the otherwise barren soils of the desert. The women cooked, weaved baskets, and made jewelry from beads made from clay and other natural resources. This tribe of Indians was so innovative; they started their own trade route, bartering needed supplies and goods from other Indian tribes in the West.

By the 1800s, the pioneers were trailblazing their way toward the Southwest in search of gold and other mining opportunities. In 1876, John James Thompson was the first pioneer to settle in Oak Creek Canyon. Over the next few years, other settlers trickled into the area, and by 1890, there were fifteen families calling Oak Creek Canyon home. Of those families, the Schneblys proved to be an influential force in what would be the eventual city of Sedona.

How Sedona Got Its Name

Sedona is named after Sedona Schnebly, a hard-working pioneer woman who came to Oak Creek Canyon to settle down with her husband, Carl. Both Sedona and Carl came from wealthy families and were well educated. However, Sedona's father disapproved of Carl and threatened that if the two were to marry, she would be cut out of the will and disinherited. Sedona's love for Carl was strong, just like her character, and she would not be swayed. On her twentieth birthday, Sedona defiantly married Carl, much to her father's chagrin.

In 1901, newlyweds Sedona and Carl moved from Gorin to Oak Creek Canyon with their two children, Elsworth and Pearl, to get away from family problems. Carl's brother, Elsworth, lived on a ranch and invited them to make a new life in the canyon. The family fit in well with the other settlers and the couple was hopeful that their new surroundings would bring them and their two children some well-deserved happiness.

Carl was an innovative man and he realized there was a need for a post office in the area. As it was, the mail took months to reach the small settlement since there were no larger towns around it. If the inhabitants of the area were to have their own post office, then the mail would come directly to them, shaving weeks off of their wait time. Carl applied for a postal permit, but he had to submit a name for the settlement in Oak Creek Canyon. At first, he decided on "Schnebly Station." However, the name was rejected because it would not fit on a cancellation stamp. Again, he tried with the name "Oak Creek Crossing." That name was rejected as well. Elsworth suggested Carl name the settlement after his wife, Sedona. Finally, the name was approved and Carl became the first postmaster of Sedona on June 26, 1902.

Life was going well for the Schnebly family. Sedona had her third child, Genevieve, shortly after moving to Oak Creek Canyon. The family settled on eighty acres of land, making their own clothes and growing their own food. Carl made a living selling corn, tomatoes, watermelons, cantaloupes, squash, and cauliflower in Flagstaff. Also, he owned the general store on his property, which also housed the post office. The family built an eleven-room ranch house, which was later used as a hotel for travelers passing through from Jerome and Flagstaff. For the most part, life was hard but satisfying.

Unfortunately, tragedy struck the Schnebly family. Their young daughter, Pearl, fell off a horse while helping round up the family's cows and was trampled to death. Sedona blamed herself for the incident, falling into a deep depression, which later caused her severe health problems. Doctors told Carl that if they did not leave their home in Oak Creek Canyon, Sedona would probably die from the heartache of losing her daughter. With hopes of getting Sedona well, Carl moved his family back to Gorin. Soon after the move, Sedona became pregnant with her fourth child, Daniel. The new child gave her purpose and seemed to ease her broken heart.

In 1932, the Schneblys moved back to Sedona. Carl worked in the apple orchards, while Sedona stayed home keeping house and canning food. The couple lived a simple, relatively happy life. They were married fifty-three years. On November 13, 1951 Sedona Schnebly died. Carl died March 13, 1954 at the age of 86.

The Harmonic Convergence

Today, Sedona is known for being a metaphysical Mecca that hosts a predominantly New Age community. This is in part due to the vortexes that are said to be housed in the red rock mesas and buttes. They are prime spots for meditation and self-awareness. However, the metaphysical population in Sedona did not boom until the 1980s, with the movement inspired by the Harmonic Convergence.

In 1987, Sedona was chosen as one of the many sacred places to congregate during the Harmonic Convergence. Also known as the Planetary Awakening, the Harmonic Convergence was introduced to the metaphysical community by Jose Arguellas in 1985. Based on cycles of the Mayan calendar, his concept suggested on August 16-17, 1987, there would be a convergence of energies and frequencies that would shift the belief systems of the world forever and produce a massive spiritual awakening.

It was hypothesized that this spiritual awakening would come in the form of near apocalyptic tragedy. The energy shifts from the Harmonic Convergence would force the Earth to slip out of its "time beam" and possibly spin off its axis into space, wiping out the human race forever. Arguellas suggested there would be an increase of UFO sightings and déjà vu, which would grow exponentially as the day of the convergence got closer.

To keep the Earth and its inhabitants from mortal peril, Arguellas theorized that if the spiritually enlightened people of the world could come together to specific sacred places throughout the world to combine their energy through meditation, they could transfer a cataclysmic event into one of enlightenment, love, and harmony.

Thousands believed they had a calling to save the planet, traveling to many locations throughout the world including the pyramids in Egypt, Stonehenge in England, and the red rock terrain of Sedona. It's estimated that between 10,000-50,000 people came to Sedona for the Harmonic Convergence, coming together in prayer and meditation to heal the planet.

Many of the "New Agers" were impressed with the beautiful red mountain landscapes of Sedona and decided to move to the sacred place. This influx of the spiritually awakened citizens kicked the New Age movement in Sedona into high gear and, today, some of the best psychics and channelers of the world call Sedona home.

3

A Trip to Metaphysical Wonderland

Being a clairvoyant tarot reader comes with a certain set of misconceptions. One is that because I can gently guide other peoples' life paths in the right direction, somehow I've got my own life mapped out. Another is that I have some sort of direct connection to an all-knowing entity, which provides me with a live, blow-by-blow of the future happenings of my life, giving me an edge on the rest of you mere mortals — so that I can take over the world one email at a time or, maybe, through the website Facebook. In all cases, this could not be further from the truth.

Although my realistic fear of flying has kept me from crashing on any tropical islands with smoke monsters and time travel issues, I have not won the lottery. Nor have I been able to successfully commit to a romantic relationship lasting more than five years. Ask my ex-husband about the perfection that comes from my psychic awareness. He knows well that if I had any common sense or inclination of what was to come in my life, I would have said no to our first date and went out with his best friend instead. The point being that I have to go through all the trials and tribulations of life just like everyone else. Unfortunately, I don't have any psychic cue cards for myself. However, if you ever need a reading, I can tell you not to marry the guy at the bar. Date his best friend. He has more money.

SEDONA

Another misconception about my life is that it's a crazy-good-time full of talking to walls and entertaining spirits...as if that's all I do with my days. Well, the entertaining spirits do happen occasionally, in the form of Mexican beer and lime, whereupon I can become quite chatty and openly giddy about hand lotion or paper clips. But I digress...

Most days I wake up in a blurry haze, check my emails, eat breakfast, and then dive into my "to do list" with an ambivalent cocktail of dread and the anticipation of accomplishment. My life is not typical, but it is normal. Instead of working at a desk, I read people. It doesn't matter if they are living or dead—energy is energy. So, if I am foretelling an aspect of someone's future, or profiling a murder, it's all the same to me. People are still who they are whether they are living or a lingering imprint on a structure. But just because I can read energy and give advice, it doesn't make me any more enlightened, especially when it comes to my own life.

It just makes for uneasy conversation whenever I am casually asked what I do for a living. Most are either intrigued or frightened or a combination of both. Always, there is that uncomfortable moment, when I know the person is wondering if I'm reading them or tapping into their thoughts. It's the shifty look in their eye; the way they instinctively take a step back. Sometimes, they get over themselves and realize that I am not doing either, or they awkwardly make an excuse to end the conversation and walk away. I have come to accept both routes, and have resolved that it comes with the job. Always, there will be those who believe that being psychic means that I have tapped an intravenous line into the omnipresent and therefore can bathe in the flow of all that is powerful and good, when really, I am just like most people. I brush my teeth and sleep just like everyone else, except that I don't like pizza and that's probably much weirder than being psychic, especially since I come from a long line of Sicilian women.

Another misconception about being psychic is that I have my finger on the pulse of all things spiritually cool. I'm a "straight-shooter" kind of person and my belief systems don't waver with the metaphysical trends. I read a lot and try new things, but I steer clear of anything that seems too contrived or one-note.

So, being that I am spiritually un-cool, when I was presented with the opportunity to research and do psychic profiles on locations in Sedona, I had little awareness of its reputation as THE Spiritual Mecca of the United States. I am from Southern California, where Botox is considered a spiritual experience. I don't really take notice of those spots in the world that are supposed to solve all your problems with one deep inhalation of its magical air. I've always considered spiritual enlightenment to be a personal journey, where life's pitfalls are the backbone of personal growth and awareness, and the enlightenment comes as a by-product of that awareness. So, I was totally unprepared for what Sedona represented to most psychics and other allegedly spiritually enlightened people.

When I told a fellow psychic reader that I would have to visit Sedona, his eyes lit up and he puffed out his chest in pride (he was a Leo) stating his readings were more clear and profound in the Sedona vortexes. He said the energy there was so spiritually pure that he could channel straight from the Source. Not just from the collective unconscious, but also from the actual Source — the bringer of all life: the God Head, The Creator.

Never in my life have I professed to have a connection to the Omnipresent. However, I have a full tap into the energy source called "sarcasm" and my first inclination went toward the idea that if a psychic can profess to be channeling from the actual Source, then he can charge big bucks for a reading. I assumed that "clearer" and "more profound" were synonymous with "I will be able to pay my rent."

My psychic friend wasn't the only one with grand stories about the energy of Sedona. I was told Sedona would be the place for my spiritual awakening. I would never feel anything like the vortexes and it would change me forever. I would become a more positive spiritual being and glisten with the light of goodness. This place called Sedona was starting to sound more and more like a trip to the Wizard of Oz and I took note to buy some really stellar red shoes. Maybe I would bring along a little lap dog in a wicker picnic basket.

Perplexed and intrigued by Sedona, I asked my roommate, Rudy, who has studied the metaphysical with an avid obsession, if he would like to spend a weekend traveling with me to experience the alleged spiritual awakening that is Sedona. I told him the stories that I had heard. Plus, he had a few to tell me, all with the same premise — Sedona *equals* spiritual awesomeness. Rudy explained that his mother, Gail, had a friend who lived in Cornville, fifteen minutes outside of Sedona, and, with his mother, he would try to arrange a sightseeing excursion since they had been to Sedona many times. Also, being a two-time, first place winner of the four-corner banjo tournament, Rudy believed he could get a gig in one of the pubs in Sedona. At the very least our trip would be musically entertaining and that wasn't so bad.

Weeks later, with a trip finally planned, Rudy and I packed our suitcases and his banjo into his green car and forged our way onto the I-10 from Tucson to the land of Spiritual Awesomeness. Hoping that we would have that profound experience that didn't include the mass consumption of locally brewed beer (and avid conversation about paper clips), we secretly prepared ourselves for the possibility that Sedona would not live up to its reputation.

Our first stop would be just outside of Phoenix to pick up Gail and to transfer our luggage into her more comfortable red PT Cruiser for the last two hours of traveling. Surprised by the lusciousness of the rugged landscape, I spent most of the trip staring out the window at the expansive trees jutting out of the green rolling hills. Green is not a color associated with the dusty, flatness of Tucson and I was amazed that the desert held more wonders than brittle tumbleweeds and prickly cacti that were my typical surroundings.

We arrived in Cornville late in the afternoon. It was a small, affluent community built around a giant neon Wal-Mart sign, the store being the only viable food-shopping source for a good twenty miles. I guess convenient in Cornville meant getting to eat at all. There were no smart, economical shopping comparisons or gourmet splurging. You shopped at the big, white sign or you ate tumbleweed-squirrel soup.

Secretly, I wondered if the Cornville Wal-Mart were run by the same entity as the South Park Wal-Mart. I half-expected to witness a mass of wild-eyed, half-crazed Cornvillagers stumbling into the store for middle-of-the-night, three-pack savings on fluffy bunny slippers. In that moment, I decided that I would keep my ears peeled for any overly-enthusiastic comments about the savings at Wal-Mart.

Originally called "Pitchner Place," according to post office records, Cornville was established in 1887. There is some discrepancy suggesting that Cornville may have been established in 1885, but this is based on the memory of old settlers in the area. Either way, the Verde Valley settlement derived its name from a paperwork error. Early pioneers opted to name their settlement Cohnville, after the Cohn family, who were one of the first to settle in the area. However, the post office misread the hand-printed name as "Cornville" and the settlers decided to keep it rather than go through the whole application process a second time.

Today, the bedroom community has a population of around 3,500, the most famous being Senator John McCain. Media called his home the "Sedona Cabin" and it's where he and Alaska Governor Sarah Palin prepared for their presidential debates.

Driving through a desolate, windy road littered with cattle grates, we neared a large hill with a giant white house dolloped at the top like a blob of sour cream. This would be our living quarters: a glorious off-white dwelling with behemoth panoramic windows that spanned the entire left side. Looking out the windows, views of the rugged, oxidized mountains of Sedona lined the horizon with a rusty glow. Though modern and pristine, the house, with its bleak walls sparse of decoration and the statuesque panes of glass peering over the expansive landscape, had me wondering if I had become a gigantic gold fish swimming around in an immaculate fish bowl.

The house belonged to Drusilla,* a screenplay writer. She also owned a kennel of dogs that ate oatmeal cookies before they were put to bed. Her daughter, Spike,* also resided in the house and had her own set of oatmeal-cookie-eating canines.

As Gail parked at the entrance of the garage, we got out of the car and exchanged polite greetings. We dragged our luggage into the house, unpacked our belongings, and then sat around the kitchen table (politely) eating gourmet pizza. The sun had set and the large panoramic windows reflected the blackness outside. Street lights were not a necessity in Cornville, much like the void of retail choice, and apparently good cell phone reception from the lack of bars on my phone.

That night would be our first excursion into Sedona to watch Rudy play banjo at a local brewery. We packed into Drusilla's white Toyota truck, as she was our official new tour guide for the trip. On the ride into town I sat in the backseat. Without street lamps carving out a path, the darkness clouded my vision, turning the mountain ranges into silver lines etched into the black. Shapes and blobs danced across the landscape as we drove down a desolate road that took us into Sedona. Even though I couldn't see the terrain, I wondered if I would be able to experience a spiritual awakening just by breathing in the air. Essentially, that's what a vortex was — just really special air, right? I breathed in deeply, hoping to feel something, but the only thing I felt was a headache coming on from the long day of traveling.

When we got to the pub, I climbed out of the car into a dirt parking lot. I was told to watch out for snakes since it was the serpent season. My blood curdled, and for a moment I contemplated getting back into the car and hiding out where it was safe from reptiles without legs. I am a city girl — a lover of pavement, sidewalks, and indoor plumbing. Snakes and other affiliates of the wilderness weren't in my repertoire. My idea of "roughing it" is not being able to find a WiFi connection for my laptop (which I couldn't find by the way). Luckily, I mustered some bravado and trudged forward, focusing on the twinkly lights of the brewery patio instead of contemplating an impending face-to-face encounter with a scaly, legless creature.

Inside, the brewery was a small, confined space, packed with tall, round wooden tables surrounded by bar stools. We sat in the corner, with large pressurized vats of beer at our backs. Rudy played with a touring blue-grass band he had met in Tucson. While the music massaged my ears and the free popcorn sated my stomach, I didn't feel anything profound. I just felt tired and even though I was having fun, I hoped that I would be able to get in my pajamas soon and get a good night's sleep for the next day's excursion.

Rudy and I slept on separate cream-colored leather couches situated in the center of the living room, right at the heart of the fish bowl. I listened to meditation CDs to fall asleep and keep me distracted from the urges of creepy midnight runs to Wal-Mart for a three-pack of "Police Academy 2," and the threat that I had become someone's new pet. Even through meditation, I secretly feared that a giant person would sneak up on me in the middle of the night and tap the tall windows of our living quarters with his fat, sausage-like fingers. That would teach me a lesson for all those times that I had tormented my own gold fish. So, you see, being me is not a profoundly enlightening experience. I am more equipped with pop-culture paranoia spawned from hours of television than impacting epiphanies brought on by clairvoyance.

Luckily, I woke the next morning sans gills, and after grazing and showering, we headed out to Sedona during the daytime, where I could behold its beauty in Technicolor. This time, our crew piled into the PT Cruiser and took Route 89A into Sedona. The jagged red rock formations towered above us, filling me with a majestic awe that left me feeling like my peon-of-a-life was insignificant in comparison to the millions of years it took for those mountains to reach their peak.

The Sedona landscape took over five million years to form, alternately being a coastal plain and an ocean bottom, creating sedimentary layers of sandstone. Dinosaurs roamed the area for 65-200 million years. No one knows why they became extinct in the area. However, for 20-65 million years, in Arizona, the landscape was severely changed by uplifts and wind erosion. From 12-20 million years ago, volcanic eruptions further formed the mountains turning the Verde Valley into a down fault with a deep basin and lakebeds. This created the Mogollin Rim, which runs two hundred miles across Yavapai County eastward to near the border of New Mexico. Around three million years ago, the Colorado Plateau uplifted, while wind and rain eroded the sedimentary formations, until they dipped into what is now Oak Creek Canyon.

Somewhere off Highway 89A, near the intersection to Highway 179, our first stop was a cute little metaphysical shop nestled alongside the babbling waters of Oak Creek. The shop seemed to be a two-story, wooden house converted into a business. It held a certain rural charm that only can be found in wooded areas rich with pioneer history. Large trees hovered over the establishment covering it in shade. That should have been my first clue that not everything in Sedona was surrounded by the eminent rays of divine goodness. We parked in another dirt lot and walked toward the metaphysical shop. The door jangled with the distinct ring of brass bells as I pushed it open. Inside the shop, a small hallway opened up to a larger room. Beyond the open space there were other rooms twisting and turning like a catacomb of merchandise. To the left there was a staircase that led somewhere that only employees could wander, and to the right, a wall of flyers and business cards for a slurry of psychics and readers that provided New Age services.

I walked through the various rooms in the shop, picking up crystals and baubles, checking out price tags with large numbers on them that didn't correlate with the relatively inexpensive object in my hand. I looked for books about ghost stories in Sedona or anything with a supernatural slant, but came up empty. Finally, deep in the labyrinth of the shop, I spotted a dark-haired woman sitting behind a desk. The desk held computer, a phone, and a myriad of office supplies. The woman had good posture, her blown-straight hair shiny, and dark business attire made her seem important and official.

Politely, I explained to the woman that I was researching haunted locations in the area for a book I was writing. Did she know of any haunted locations in Sedona or were there any books I could find to lead me in the right direction? Immediately, the woman sized me up, looking me up-and-down to make sure that I was worthy enough for conversation. I felt like Julia Roberts hoofing it in Beverly Hills in a trashy outfit with thigh-high-boots. Glancing down at my jeans and blouse, I sighed with relief. I had not forgotten to put clothes on today, and my underwear was exactly where they should be, hidden from view. Still, I couldn't shake the feeling I had failed the super-cool-spiritual-test and the woman's response was going reflect my grade. For a moment, I wondered why this metaphysical shop suddenly reminded me of high school.

With attitude bleeding through every word, the official-looking woman explained to me that she was the receptionist who booked readings for the shop's many psychics. If I wanted to know any information about hauntings or ghosts in Sedona, I would have to get a reading and perhaps the psychic could give me that information if I were to ask. However, that is all the help she could give me.

I blinked a few times, tilting my head in confusion. Did she just tell me that I had to *pay* a psychic to find out about the ghost stories in Sedona? Maybe the meanings of my words were misconstrued. Maybe she thought I wanted to talk to ghosts or that I needed to talk to someone dead. Although I was pretty sure I spoke in sentences that conveyed a straightforward meaning, I gave the haughty woman the benefit of the doubt. Again, I reiterated I was writing a book, and I was looking for research materials or stories about the haunted areas in Sedona. This time, the woman directly stared me in the face, inhaling deeply from the bottom of her toes and blew out an exasperated breath. She proceeded to tell me that without a psychic booking she couldn't do anything to help me. With that, she turned toward her computer, disregarding my presence like I wasn't there.

At that moment I realized the metaphysical had nothing to do with spirituality in Sedona — it was big business. I would not find my happy-place in Sedona. It would not awaken any part of my being. It would not inspire me. However, it would remind me that enlightenment is a personal journey on an isolated road, and not a one-time trip to Metaphysical Wonderland, no matter how majestic its mountain or how magical its air.

The Ann Miller Residence

Perhaps the most notorious haunted house in Sedona belonged to acclaimed film actress Ann Miller. A dancer and actress, Miller was known for her roles in the MGM musicals "Kiss Me Kate," "Easter Parade," and "On the Town." She was famed for her speed in tap dancing — film publicists claimed she could tap five hundred taps per minute.

Miller was born Johnnie Lucille Ann Collier because her father wanted a boy, but her parents often called her Annie. As a child, Ann suffered from rickets, a bone disease caused by malnutrition that softens the bones resulting in fractures and deformity. She started dance classes to help strengthen her bone density and ended up becoming a dance prodigy.

By lying about being of adult age, at age 11, Miller worked as a dancer at the Black Cat Club in San Francisco, where she was discovered by Lucille Ball and talent scout Benny Rubin. In 1936, a thirteen-year-old (again lying about being 18) Ann Miller signed a contract with RKO. She stayed with the production company for four years, until 1940 when she was picked up by Columbia Pictures. In the following years she would make the MGM musicals that made her a household name.

In the 1940s, Ann Miller invented pantyhose as a solution to constantly having to replace her nylons. It was common practice for dancers to have their thigh-high nylons sewn to their undergarments to keep them in place. If the nylons tore they had to be completely stripped from the undergarments and a new pair sewn in its place. As a time saver, Miller requested that the hosiery company make her single pantyhose.

Later in her career, Miller was known for her signature black bouffant hairstyle and her red lipstick. Her costumes emphasized her svelte figure and her long legs. In 1956, her film career ended, but she was active on Broadway for the next twenty years. Miller is best known for starring in "Mame" in 1969 and "Sugar Babies" with Mickey Rooney in 1979. She won the prestigious Sarah Siddons Award in 1983 for her role in "Sugar Babies." Ann Miller died of lung cancer at the age of eighty. Her star is on the Hollywood Walk of Fame at 6914 Hollywood Boulevard in Hollywood California.

Ann Miller was a spiritualist who studied psychic phenomenon and astrology. She wrote a book called *Tapping into the Force*, an autobiography about her living with psychic abilities. Miller researched her past lives, resonating with Egyptian history and archeology. She believed she was Queen Hathshepsut of Egypt in a former life.

Ann Miller bought a getaway house in Sedona. She divided her time between there and her main residence in Beverly Hills (where she died). Using her own psychic abilities, Miller claimed a fierce Native American warrior haunted her Sedona house. Ann asked a Hopi shaman to assist with a house clearing. From the shaman, she learned that the structure had been owned by an early pioneer whose son had died during the construction. The man believed the house to be haunted by his son, and had it blessed by an Indian tribal chief to stop the paranormal activity. Unfortunately, the blessing did not stick and the structure remained haunted much to the chagrin of Ann Miller, who bought the house not aware of its history of paranormal activity.

According to the shaman, the house was built on sacred ground where there was an Indian kiva. The tribal ritual performed by the Indian chief for the pioneer activated the fierce Native American warrior to guard over the sacred place. After Ann Miller received the information about her home, she had the grounds exorcised and blessed. According to Miller, after the exorcism, the house remained free of paranormal activity.

4

VORTEXES

Sedona is famously known for its vortexes. A Vortex is a whirling, spiraling energy field funneling from the surface of the earth. It creates a small residual magnetic field at the strongest point. Juniper trees are thought to respond to the vortex energy by growing in a helical spiral or an axial twist. Around most of the vortexes you can witness the base of the trees twisting in a clockwise direction.

Vortexes in Sedona are said to be points of concentrated spiritual energy that span multiple dimensions. When submerged in a vortex, the concentrated spiritual energy is said to aid you in merging with your personal self, awakening truth and enlightenment from within. Sometimes, during this awakening you are forced to deal with core issues that bring out your shadow self such as fear, anger, and anxiety. When confronted, these problems can be resolved, which will inevitably merge both sides of your psyche, creating balance and harmony. Even though sometimes the experience may present painful realizations, ultimately, bathing in the energy of a vortex will reap positive benefits — and fill your life with self-awareness and understanding.

The term "vortex" was coined by trance medium, Page Bryant. During her stay in Sedona, she channeled information that stated there were electromagnetic fields in the red rocks that were spiritual in nature. Bryant was

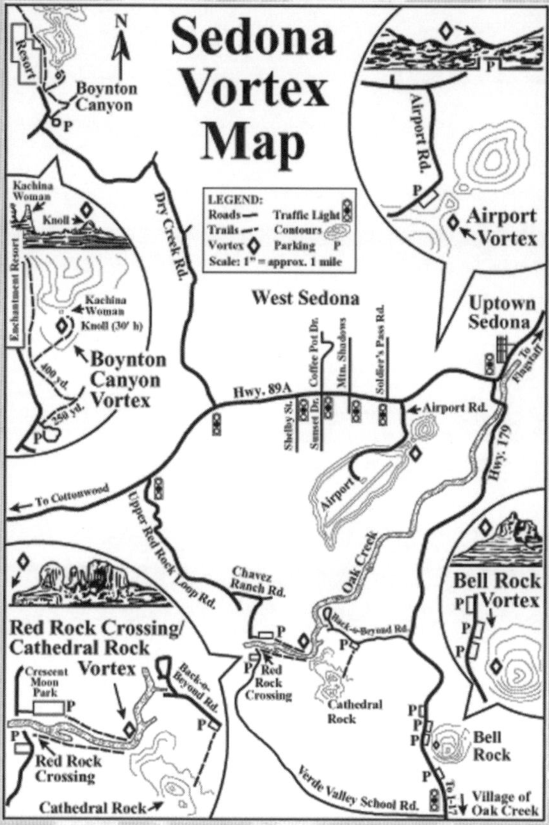

led to certain areas and meditated there to confirm her impressions. Her channeling became clearer and she had positive physical responses to the areas. She cited there were four main vortexes in Sedona: Bell Rock, Cathedral Rock, Boynton Canyon, and Airport Vortex.

Bell Rock

Directions: From Phoenix, take I-17 north to Highway 179 (exit 298). Turn left onto Highway 179 and follow it passed the Village of Oak Creek. Bell Rock should be on the right. Pass Bell Rock and turn right into the parking lot. There will be a trail leading to the vortex ion the right.

Bell Rock is said to be the strongest vortex in Sedona and can be felt in the whole area not just on the rock itself. Bell Rock balances and strengthens both the masculine and feminine side of self.

The name, Bell Rock, is due to the bell-like shape of the mountain, and because it's supposed to "tone" your spiritual energies, harmonizing them into balance. There are stronger spots as you climb the large rock formation. However, you don't need to be on Bell Rock to feel its circular energy.

By John and Micki Baumann. Copyright © Deva Designs.

Many believe the rock formation's high electromagnetic field is like a beacon signaling to spiritual beings in other dimensions as well as life on other planets. If you touch the rock while meditating, you may be contacted by spirits that lead you into a higher level of understanding, harmony, and balance. UFO sights are prevalent near the rock formation.

Bloody Bell Rock

With Drusilla at the wheel and Gail sitting sidekick, Rudy, Spike, and I sat in the backseat of the PT Cruiser admiring the massive rust-colored rock mesas on either side of us. When I say "admiring," what I really mean is that I was feeling mighty small, like a crab picking at bits of brine at the bottom of a vast ocean canyon. It was a fine feeling as long as I didn't look up or focus on anything but the headrest of the back seat. If I really concentrated on the oxidized landscape, anxiety twitched in my stomach and my hands began to sweat. I wondered if I was beginning to get car sick or maybe I just didn't like feeling miniscule like a sea scavenger in the ocean called life.

Traveling down Highway 179, Bell Rock came up on our left. It was easy to spot because of its obvious bell-like shape on the horizon. Continuity is a great thing. Drusilla explained that as you approach Bell Rock, you should start to feel the energy from the vortex. Even though I wasn't too keen on the whole magical air concept, I put my skepticism in check and opened my senses so that I could fully experience the energy around me.

The way I read energy is by pulling it into my aura, interpreting it, and then recycling it back out. I don't hold on to the impressions or feelings I receive. It's a constant flow of energy coming in and being forced out, kind of like a filtering system on a fish tank. I am the charcoal and the impurities are the impressions I am receiving. Usually, impressions come out of order; the images with the strongest impact come first and then everything following in descending order of sensation. As the impressions are brought forward, I talk them out in pieces until they begin to fit together like a puzzle. The more time I have to sit with the information, the more the whole situation comes into focus. If I only have a few minutes, then the information will be precise, but may seem random like a nose without a face.

As I took in the vortex air, I started to feel something, but it wasn't happy or harmonious like all of the experiences I had been told or read about on

BELL ROCK TR.
BELL ROCK PATH
COURTHOUSE LOOP

the Internet. Actually, what I was feeling was sort of sinister and foreboding — and it *wasn't* coming from Bell Rock. It was coming from the landscape on the right. I was sitting on the right side of the car, so the easiest energy for me to pull from was on that side because my body naturally shifted in that direction. Still, I can pull from many areas at once, for miles at a time. However, the most prominent and traumatic impressions came from the monstrous red rock formations on my right side.

I took a deep breath, trying to keep the anxiety at bay. Stills of time were flashing in front of my third eye like a slide show. There were dwellings carved into the mountains from a peaceful Indian tribe that resided here. The Indians were watching me watching them; curiously, some Indians poked their heads out from their caves while others stood precariously on small ledges etched into the side of the mountain, leaning against the rock for balance. They stared at me, intently, wanting to convey their story me.

In my mind, I asked, "What happened here?"

In response, the mountains turned crimson with blood and hundreds of bodies, broken and flayed, canvassed the cliffs. I flinched and my stomach flip-flopped.

I remember saying, "These mountains are red because of all the bloodshed in the soil, not because of oxidation."

Rudy laughed sardonically. He thought it was funny that I could not feel the powerful healing powers of the vortex, but instead was experiencing blood and carnage. It would be just like me to turn something positive into a blood bath.

Rudy asked me how I came up with the conclusion that the mountains were dipped in blood. I told him I saw two Indian tribes battling each other in the mountains. The cave dwellers were peaceful and benign. They were farmers and traders, and lived a quiet, resourceful life. Another tribe settled in, Nomads, and ambushed the cave dwellers, wiping them out. They had not been prepared for battle. It was not their way of life. The Nomad tribe was savage and blood-thirsty — killing just to kill.

I could smell the warm blood in the air; the thick, metallic taste of it clung to my tongue. It made me want to retch and my palms sweat. I felt the cold fear of the cave dwellers as they were massacred. Anxiety curled at my insides and I wanted desperately to get out of the area so that the images of carnage would disappear.

As I finished describing my impressions to my fellow car passengers, Drusilla said she wasn't surprised at my reaction to the area. She said that it was common for psychics to pick up on the feeling of bloodshed near Bell Rock, especially when the vortex was strong. In a way, I was relieved that I wasn't going crazy and there were others that had picked up on the same impressions. Still, I was a little miffed that only the positive attributes of the Sedona vortexes were published on the web and in pamphlets proclaiming them to be sacred spots for divine intervention. While these spots may very well hold a special energy with mysterious spiritual qualities, it seems tainted by the harsh realities of the human experience. The lives of those who settled in the canyon had put their bloody mark on the walls of the rugged cliffs, changing its molecular structure forever.

You Spin Me Right Round

You would think after the less than stellar experience I had with Bell Rock the first time, at some point my instinct of self-preservation would kick in and keep me from being a repeat offender. However, I have a "writer's memory," which involves repressing the bad parts of an experience and then revising it with an elaborate concoction of fantasy that seems much more interesting in my head. It makes for eloquent retellings of tales (since I tend to believe my own delusions), but it's not so helpful in the turn of reality.

And that's how I ended up sitting in the passenger seat of a blue Dodge Durango with Stacy, tech chick for P.I.S.A. Paranormal, driving frenetically on Interstate 17 to revisit Bell Rock in its entire horrific splendor. Kendra, a paranormal investigator-in-training, sat behind me on the right side and Marcus, an exchange student from Singapore, sat to the left.

In this paranormal tale, everyone fits, except the exchange student, and that theme would run the course of the whole weekend excursion. Being that he had no interest in the supernatural, and actually disagreed with the idea of it due to his own religious beliefs, it seemed rather odd to take him on an excursion where ghosts were the main theme, but he wanted to go because he was sick of looking at the flat, dry lands of Tucson and longed for adventure.

However, his idea of adventure and mine were somewhat at odds with each other. His "spirited" demeanor brimmed with the kind of boundless energy reserved for youth or wire-haired terriers. Marcus

wanted to hike to the top of mountains and rigorously climb hills. He wanted to run and leap and catch rabbits. Okay, no, that would be the terrier. However, the metaphor fits in terms of his enthusiasm.

My idea of adventure was to sit passively and wait for something interesting to come to me. If nothing happened, then I would head to our hotel room to sleep until my headache went away. Partly this could have been due to my birthday-binge-drinking the night before. The idea of being thirty-five hit me hard and I went into a bit of a mortal tailspin.

Again, one would think working within the realm of the spiritual on a daily basis would keep me from a birthday-induced-mini-life crisis. However, my ego is alive and thriving and sometimes it takes captain of the helm. This is how I ended up knocking back drinks to ease the impending anxiety of my mortality. I remember being in a restaurant and ordering food, but I took the food home and drank my dinner instead. Needless to say, it was an eventful birthday, and much to my chagrin, the fun caught up with me the next morning.

Still, there was work that had to be done and most importantly pictures that needed to be taken for the book. During my last excursion to the land of magical air, there was promise of pictures and other fantastical musings. Much like Sedona, the talk far outweighed the reality. There were no pictures; just emails with polite refusals and reputations that needed be protected. Steam came out of my ears and then anxiety washed over as the fear caught in my throat.

Lucky for me, I have impetuous friends with photography skills who are always up for last-minute road trips. Still, the stress of having no pictures for my book and my birthday looming over me like a death shroud could have possibly persuaded me to overlook the alcohol consumption the night before. So, despite my throbbing head and my wobbly ego, I took a shower, hoping to wash the sleep from by body and keep focused on the task at hand.

Beef jerky is the cure for all, especially when it's spicy and brimming with red pepper. I gnawed on a slab of jerky on our way to Sedona. The hotness on my tongue felt good as it spread to my sinuses making my eyes water and my nose run. I felt fuzzy and tingly inside. I speak of the beef jerky because it was probably the most interesting thing that happened on our four-hour car trip.

The conversation in the car was minimal because we all had experienced the "fun" from the night before and now were paying the price. Well, except Marcus who was revved up like a muscle car engine and rearing to go. However, his excitement turned into boredom halfway through the drive. At one point, I looked to over to catch him with his eyes closed and his head leaning against the glass of the car window.

Again, our first stop in Sedona would be Bell Rock. This time I was in the driver's seat since Stacy needed to get some schoolwork done. Most of the trip she was quiet, staring at her laptop in furtive concentration. Kendra didn't say much either, and bored Marcus slept. Yes, we were that exciting.

For those who are directionally challenged, let me just warn you that downtown Sedona is not the place to exercise a spirit of adventure. There are confusing roundabouts that don't have any logical practicality to them and the location is littered with roadwork. A lot of lanes are sparkly road deflectors that twist and wind into a tight, cramped labyrinth of non-directional agony and torture. I'm pretty sure Dante had Sedona roadwork in mind when he wrote about the rings of hell.

According to a website dedicated to updating travelers on the road construction in Sedona, the work is supposed to be completed early 2009. As I write this, it *is* early 2009 and the roads were still a mind-boggling mess. I advise going to the Sedona Information website at www. sedonainformation.com/road_conditions.php or call the road condition telephone service at 888-411-7623 (411-ROAD) to get updates on the construction before you make your trip to Sedona. There are helpful hints and alternate routes to take so that you can avoid driving around in the confusion.

The roundabouts are especially tedious because they are in the midst of the chaotic construction. The direction of traffic does not flow like a normal roundabout and can be tricky to navigate even for those who are used to them. The point being, enter downtown Sedona at your own risk or call ahead and be prepared.

Our posse circled around the Highway 89A and Highway 179 junction a few times, debating on which way to travel due to the road construction; we turned left, reached a dead end, and then went the opposite way on Highway 89A. That took us through a very rural, winding road between ragged ridges of red mountains. Finally, we turned around one more time, veered through a tight lane created by street deflectors, and turned right on Highway 179. We hugged the curves of the faux lane at sloth speed anxiously hoping that we were finally going the right way. After what seemed like a lifetime in suspended animation, we finally turned a corner and Bell Rock was in our view on our left side. Blowing out a breath that I didn't know I was holding, I calmed down, realizing we were finally close to our destination.

The parking lot to Bell Rock was a little bit tricky to find because I had to cross over the other side of Highway 179 to get to it. We came into Sedona from Cottonwood instead of Phoenix, so my directions were backwards. I had thought it would be easier from the opposite direction since I didn't have to dodge traffic from the other side of the highway. Like most things in my life, I have to do everything the hard way.

Riding on a little bit of faith and instinct, I passed over the highway and entered into the mouth of the parking lot. The lot was bigger than I expected and there were many tourists and hikers heading to the trail that led to Bell Rock. I parked the Durango and the four of us headed toward the trail. The silt on the uphill path was powdered with a soft red dust that clung to our shoes. It was a short ten-minute walk through a small trail that opened up the large, red-rock formation.

At the base of Bell Rock, bicyclists and hikers littered the trails that circled around the formation. Enthusiastic outdoor types climbed up Bell Rock, hoping to reach the top plateau that was hard to see with the naked eye. Stacy, Kendra, and I decided to settle near the bottom of the rock. Markus asked if he could hike to the top of Bell Rock with all the other well-adjusted people who had probably slept. We set him free and he bounded forward with the excitable energy of a Labrador chasing a red ball. It was a decision that would later have us contemplating who would be eaten first if we, in fact, got stuck on Bell Rock for the night. I can assure you it would not have been me. In crisis situations, I am cool as a cucumber and would have no problem eating my friends for survival. It's the Sicilian blood in me.

According to some reports, Bell Rock is supposed to have a strong electromagnetic field that can be recorded. Stacy brought along her electromagnetic field detector and infrared ambient thermometer combo to test that theory. We sat down and set up the gadget between us on a flat part of rock to see if there were any abnormal fluctuations in temperature or EMF. The temperature stayed constant.

I lay back against the rock to get a feel for its energy. It was a nice warm day with a slight breeze. The sky bled azure with streaks of billowy white. I closed my eyes hoping to put myself into a somewhat meditative state, but Bell Rock was not a mindful place. Hikers constantly walked up the path, and helicopters providing sightseeing excursions circled the area every few minutes. Add that to the whirring of bicycles and the constant flow of traffic on the highway down below. It was a quiet cacophony of rhythms and actions that made it hard to go within and find my center. I was amazed at the stories of channelers and psychics who had come to Bell Rock and were able to connect to spirits. How were they able to drown out the all the sound of the outside world?

Luckily, I had not slept a lot the night before, so my body quieted faster than usual. I felt heavy and relaxed, and soon my mind stilled. Quietly, I laid there for a little while, hoping to get in touch with a spirit or a have a profound meditation experience. Nothing happened. Mostly, I just fought sleep. But just in case, I said a prayer for my family and friends. Also, I asked that parts of me become balanced and more harmonious per the claims of Bell Rock.

I sat up and let my eyes adjust to the light. Stacy and Kendra were milling about being curious. I asked if there had been any weird EMF or temperature readings while I was pretending to meditate. Stacy said there hadn't been anything unusual; just some mild fluctuations that were within normal range.

Feeling lazy, I didn't get up from my spot and watched the commotion all around me. After a while I realized that every few minutes there was a whooshing feeling that spun around me. It only happened for a few seconds and then it would go away. In that moment, the air felt like it spun around in a giant circle moving everything with it. I wondered if it was my hangover or if it was a true sensation.

I asked Stacy if she was feeling anything weird. She said that she wasn't sure, but every few minutes she felt a spinning sensation. She attributed to being tired and hung-over. I told her I was feeling the same thing.

We decided to sit next to each other and, when the feeling came upon us again, we would check the EMF detector for anomalies. Within a few minutes, the dizzying feeling came back. I looked over at Stacy and she thought she felt it too. She looked at the EMF detector and it spiked. As soon as the feeling left, the EMF went back to normal. We waited for the feeling to happen again; when it did, the EMF spiked like the last time. The third time, we realized we were onto something.

I'm not sure why the swirling motion raised the electromagnetic field of Bell Rock. I could only guess that the turning movement was the vortex. When the sensation did hit, it felt like it was moving in a clockwise direction. Maybe there was something to the idea of a vortex being a conical energy, but how or what it did to the human body was not explained. How could one say that the elevated electromagnetic fields raised spiritual awareness or harmonized the male and female energies of your body? Perhaps it's like Hoodoo or other faith-based paths. Perhaps you have to believe in it for it to work.

After a while, Stacy, Kendra, and I were tired and hungry. We decided to take a short trip to the Chapel of the Holy Cross, and then go somewhere for dinner. This plan was foiled by the fact that we couldn't find Markus. We had been on Bell Rock for over an hour, and we had no sight of him, but we figured he would be back soon. Another hour went by and the sun started to drop against the horizon. The sun would be setting soon and the warmth gave way to a cool breeze. Frustrated, we called his name and walked around a little bit to find him. We didn't want to go far in fear of getting lost or not being there when he came back. Hunger pains and low blood sugar took its toll. Soon we were eyeing each other suspiciously. Who would be the first to be eaten?

Luckily, dire decisions were not needed because Markus finally came back. The only way to get to the top of Bell Rock is by circling it. He had gotten to the top, and then lost his sense of direction. Gripped with anxiety, he hastily tried to get down the mountain and got further lost. Fortunately, he stumbled upon a group of hikers who showed him back to the base of Bell Rock where we were grumpily waiting for him. Lucky for him, the Donner Party banter had only gone to the steps of conceptualization and nobody had to be sacrificed for the sake of survival. Although, we vowed to never let Markus out of our sight again. All that boundless energy only got him into trouble because, unfortunately, he didn't have wisdom or foresight. Also, he was directionally challenged. We trudged back to the car and found a bag of snacks. It would hold us over until we got to Jerome.

Although I am still skeptical of the magical power of the vortex, there is an interesting side note to my second visit to Bell Rock. A couple of weeks later, I was grappling with some emotional issues. My natural inclination is to rationalize my feelings until they make sense and then I can express them clearly. I'm not good at letting go and just feeling things as they come. I have to understand them and understand why or where they are coming from. It seems comical that personally I am not able to trust my own emotional reactions to things, especially since in readings I am clear about others paths based on those same emotional responses. Though, with me, it's a bit like not being able to see the forest for the trees. It's always hard when you are in the thick of things.

While all of this emotional upheaval was stirring, the left side of my face broke out. I don't regularly have face blemishes and I thought it was odd. A few days later, I had a fever blister break out only on the left side of my mouth. Then, I slit my left thumb open on the crease of my thumbnail. It was a deep cut and my thumb swelled up for a week.

The left side of your body represents the feminine side of self. It deals with emotions, sensitivity, intuition, and trusting emotional responses. It seemed too coincidental that I was fighting my own intuition at the time. My emotional responses to my situation were wildly out of control, even though my instincts were telling me to step outside of myself and get an objective point of view. I ignored my intuition and my situation turned from bad to worse. I was definitely having trouble with my feminine side. From that experience, I learned a valuable lesson about how I deal with personal relationships. On reflection, I realized what my core issue was and how I needed to take steps in order to cope with it.

In hindsight, I thought about my time on Bell Rock. I did ask to be harmonized and balanced in my meditation. Perhaps, my outbreak and emotional breakdown was a way of bringing up issues that needed to be resolved in order to become a more balanced person. Perhaps, I was being forced to work more with my feminine side and trust my emotional responses instead of countering them with anger and logic. At the end of the drama, I did feel more like both sides of myself were working more harmoniously.

I still wonder if that meditation was the catalyst for the events. Or if the energy was already set in motion and it was just a coincidence that I thought about it on the rock formation. In either case, all of my experiences in Sedona impacted me in some way. Whether it was positive or negative, the red rocks hold an intrigue that can't be explained.

AIRPORT VORTEX

Directions: At the intersection of Highways 179 and 89A, turn left on Highway 89A and drive west for one mile. Turn left at Airport Road. Drive for about a half-mile and turn left into the parking lot.

The Airport Vortex strengthens the masculine side of self: self-confidence, internal strength, risk-taking, taking control of one's life, and decision-making. Its energy balances the physical body and opens the chakras. The Airport Vortex enhances psychic energies and altered states of consciousness.

The Headache Vortex

Needless to say, after my initial experience with the Bell Rock vortex, my desire to experience the other vortexes dwindled to one of obligatory research and that, coupled with the drug-dealer-like insinuations (money exchanged for information) from the well-coiffed receptionist at the metaphysical store, had my hackles up in a big way. All illusions had been dispelled. Sedona seemed like a trite pit of pretentiousness disguised by pretty scenery. I wanted to get back to my supernaturally un-cool, dusty world of cacti and flat, brown symmetry. However, I kept my restless feelings to myself and proceeded onward to the next spot.

Drusilla drove us west on Highway 89A. She decided we would travel to a special place in the Boynton Canyon vortex that she loved because of the beautiful scenery and the way it made her feel. On the way we would be driving into the Airport vortex. Drusilla asked Rudy and me to tell her when we "felt" something. Gail and Spike were to keep to themselves since they knew where the vortex was and weren't supposed to give any hints.

Everyone became quiet. Rudy and I anticipated an energy shift. I took a deep breath to ground myself, hoping that this vortex didn't hit me with more impressions of another blood bath. A few minutes passed, and I didn't feel anything weird. I looked over at Rudy for context clues, but he was absorbed in the scenery. The terrain seemed to have changed significantly. Trees hovered over the green and red landscape of clumped bushes, brittle twigs, and shrubbery. The oxidized plateaus of Sedona were still prominently on the horizon, but they took a back seat to the dry greenery that seemed more typical of the desert. I guessed he wasn't feeling anything either or he would have noticed me staring at him.

The car veered as we approached a curve in the road. As we straightened out, my head ached and a sharp pang flitted through my third eye. The pain hit me square in the face for just a moment and, just as quickly, disappeared, like a quick shot of electricity buzzing through my head. I thought it was a strange sensation, but I figured my sinuses were adjusting to the dry weather. Or maybe I wasn't used to the higher elevation of Sedona compared to Tucson. I glanced over at Rudy one more time, but he was oblivious and stared out the window.

A few more minutes passed. Finally, Drusilla broke the silence, asking if we were feeling anything. Rudy and I made eye contact, but from his posture I knew he didn't feel anything. I told Drusilla we were not good at the guessing games and she should probably tell us when we got to the vortex, so we didn't miss it. She replied we *were* in it, and that we had been in it since just before the curve in the road. I described my lightening quick headache and told her that was the only thing I felt. She said nobody had ever heard of anyone having that sort of sensation. Lucky me. I got to be the first to experience blinding pain in a vortex. I could hardly wait to visit the next vortex and see what sort of uncomfortable affliction would be thrown upon me.

BOYNTON CANYON

Directions: At the intersection of Highway 179, make a left onto Highway 89A and drive about three miles. Turn right on Dry Creek Road and drive the route for Boynton Canyon. You'll be on it for about three miles, then turn left at the "T" intersection. Drive about 1.5 miles and turn right at the "T" intersection. Drive into the parking lot on the right. If you end up at the Enchantment Resort entrance, you have driven too far.

☠ ☠ ☠ ☠ ☠ ☠ ☠ ☠ ☠ ☠ ☠ ☠ ☠ ☠ ☠ ☠ ☠

The Boynton Canyon Vortex balances the masculine and feminine sides, strengthening intimacy, commitment, honesty, and openness. Its energies harmonize your spiritual self as well as your relationships with others. Considered to be a sacred place by the Yavapai Indians, Boynton Canyon is considered the birthplace of the first woman. She was said to be born in a cave in the canyon—and many believe she *still* resides there, helping to maintain the energy of the vortex.

Love and Light

There is an old saying, "the third time is the charm." I have found it applies to many instances in my life, including the Sedona vortexes. Near the Boynton Canyon Vortex, Drusilla drove our carload up a semi-winding road that led to a new land development. Stopping at a gate, Drusilla parked the car and we walked toward an opening that would be the entrance to the new affluent neighborhood where parcels started at $3 million dollars, which didn't include the building of an actual structure. Though streets signs were posted, back roads were paved, and lawns were sprawling, there were no houses to be found. Still, the ambience of a quiet neighborhood emanated from the surroundings, and two school-aged kids whizzed by on their bikes following the semi-circle of the streets, their shaggy dog panting behind them. A few minutes later, their dad breezed by us on foot and we exchanged greetings.

Standing in the grass, I was affronted with a heavy sensation in my chest, and I felt like it was getting hard to breathe. Since my other experiences in the vortexes weren't exactly positive, at first, I started to panic. I wondered if it was the elevation getting to me, or if this was the vortex that was, *finally,* going to do me in. I closed my eyes, inhaled deeply, and blew out slowly, taking in the energy and letting the feeling flow through me.

My insides warmed and my body tingled. I realized the heavy feeling in my chest was really from a heightened sense of euphoria, not anticipatory anxiety. I relaxed and let the rush of energy wash over me. Energy slowly swirled around me like I was in the middle of a giant funnel, but it also passed through me, recycling my energy with every breath. I felt like my life force was being merged with a greater energy force, and it almost tickled from the inside out. I wanted to reach my arms outward and grasp the air in my closed fists because it felt like it had viscosity or a weightness that didn't make sense. It was comforting and peaceful, but also uplifting and intense. Breathing seemed tougher from the density of the air, but also effortless. I was perplexed by the simple happiness that coursed through me. If I weren't careful, I would start using words like "enlightened" and "harmonious" to describe the shift in my energy.

Skepticism niggled in the back of my mind, but I pushed it away because I didn't want to give up the feeling of contentment and peacefulness that coursed through my body. I felt grounded and alive. Looking around, I asked our entourage if they were feeling the same dizzy, warm energy. We compared notes and everyone agreed we were all feeling the positive funnel of energy flowing in and around them.

Elated, I wanted to share the good energy around me. I believe that I am nothing more than the sum of all my parts and those parts consist of my family and others that I love. Closing my eyes, I tapped into the vortex energy and I thought about all the people in my life who were important to me. With good intentions, I envisioned a white light made from the pure energy swirling around them. I wished everyone happiness, health, wealth, wisdom, and love. When I opened my eyes, I felt loved and sated. Also, I thanked the gods for letting me experience something spiritual and enlightening in Sedona, so that I could understand its intrigue, and maybe begin to appreciate its charm.

CATHEDRAL ROCK

Directions: Drive west for about four miles on Highway 89A from the intersection of Highway 179. Turn left on Upper Red Rock Loop Road and drive for about two miles. Turn left on Chavez Ranch Road. Follow the pavement for about one mile and turn left into Crescent Moon Park. There is a $3 entrance fee.

Cathedral Rock strengthens the feminine side: kindness, compassion, nurturing, and maternal instincts. Its energy is strong and intense, but calming and soothing, aiding in meditation, regeneration, and enhancing intuition. The top of Cathedral Rock is at about a 1,000 feet and supposedly glows at night.

(Author's note: Due to time constraints, I did not get to go here and personally experience this vortex.)

5

Chapel of the Holy Cross

780 Chapel Road, Sedona, Arizona

Directions: Drive on Highway 179 South, toward the Village of Oak Creek, for about three miles. Turn left on Chapel Road. Drive to the end of the road.

Hours of Operation: Monday to Saturday, 9 a.m.-5 p.m.; Sunday, 10 a.m.-5 p.m.

Marguerite Brunswig Staude, a resident of Oak Creek, designed the Chapel of the Holy Cross. Staude had a reoccurring vision of putting a cross on the newly-built Empire State Building and it inspired her to become an architecture student of Frank Lloyd Wright's. With Wright's assistance, she proposed to build a skyscraper cathedral in Europe. Unfortunately, World War II broke out and her plans fell through. However, in 1955 her dream was realized when she decided to build the cathedral in her own back yard. The Chapel of the Holy Cross was completed in 1956. Now, the Roman Catholic diocese of Phoenix

SEDONA

and the Saint John Vianney Parish of Sedona, Arizona own the structure.

Nestled between two red rock formations, the Chapel of the Holy Cross sits two hundred feet aboveground. The A-framed glass window is accentuated by a ninety-foot cross wedged into the rock seemingly supporting the whole structure. The Chapel of the Holy Cross is said to have its own vortex. Many have meditated in the area experiencing visions of an underground civilization. Also, there have been many UFO sightings near the top of the rock formation where the chapel is situated.

The Eagle and the Indian Woman

We arrived at the Chapel of the Holy Cross just before the 5 p.m. church service, which made parking a nightmare. The steep, windy hill buzzed with the sound of idling engines, as eager worshippers vied for the elusive parking spot. Since our lot of passengers consisted mostly of pagans or reformed Catholics, we were in no hurry to get to the chapel. Although, I was mildly curious about how a Catholic service in Sedona was conducted.

Being from a Sicilian family on my mom's side and a WASPY family on my dad's side, I had my bouts with Catholicism in my childhood, mostly through the occasional wedding or funeral. I remember the restlessness I encountered, trying not to wiggle in the cold, hard pew. All the men wore baggy dresses and funny hats, and it took all of my will to pay attention to strings of foreign words that had no meaning to me while the sweet, thick scent of incense burned my eyes and stung my nose.

If that wasn't bad enough, at the front of the church, there was usually a depiction of Jesus on the cross — his stabbed and beaten body hanging half-clothed from nails driven into his hands and feet. A crown of thorns dug into his head and rivulets of blood trickled down his morose face. There were other statues too, their drawn faces staring solemnly into space like they had never seen a happy moment in their entire life.

These visions of torture and somberness always led me to believe that Catholicism made you unhappy and brow-beaten. If I wasn't careful to keep my wits about me, I would end up sad and lonely, or worse, nailed to a cross somewhere. Weddings at a Catholic church seem more like torture than a blessed occasion and during funerals I wasn't somber because of the death, but because I was so fidgety and uncomfortable, hoping I wasn't the next person on the Catholicism hit list.

Intellectually, I understood I was just a visitor in this macabre world where every Sunday, members ate the body and drank the blood of Christ, who happened to be in plain view, bloody and beaten, just in case anyone forgot what they were snacking on. With my vivid imagination and already well-developed paranoia, the ritual seemed oddly like cannibalism and I wondered what would happen if they ran out of Jesus parts to feed to their masses. Would they kidnap unsuspecting visiting children, drown them in the baptism pool, and use the good parts for Sunday Mass? It was better that I didn't find out, and keep my wits about me, just in case.

I shuddered, remembering my childhood anxieties, and tried to clear my head. Gail was driving this time, in her red PT Cruiser, Drusilla was in the passenger seat, and Rudy, Spike, and I resumed our sitting arrangements in the back seats. It was our last day in Sedona and we spent the day casually strolling through the overpriced metaphysical shops. Our last stop would be the Chapel of the Holy Cross to find out whether or not the vortex held any weight to its claims. So far, out of the three vortexes I had encountered, only one had lived up to the hype. The others fell flat like a warm soda. So far, the odds weren't looking too good — if I was in Vegas, I wouldn't be making any large bets.

The Chapel of the Holy Cross had one advantage only I could appreciate. I was told that if you looked over the rocky hill on the right side, you got a perfect view of the Italian-inspired mansion that belonged to Nicolas Cage. Now that's what I called a profound spiritual experience. Even better if Nick just happens to be sunbathing, but I digress...

Eventually we found a parking spot near the bottom of the winding road that led to the Chapel. We found ourselves trudging round and round, up the hill, with the rest of the tourists and churchgoers like a line of out-of-breath working ants. It's a steep climb, not advisable for anyone who is allergic to exercise that doesn't fall under the category of pounding the mall pavement at Macy's to reap the benefits of a fabulous sale. At least there's a reward with that kind of exercise; fabulousness at a fraction of its usual cost is a great motivator. However, climbing up a hill to get to the top? Well, I leave it to those who eat granola bars and like endorphin rushes that doesn't include a forty percent off sale on shoes. This girl will just stick to her retail exercise regimen. Eventually, I made it to the top of the hill and after sitting a spell on the rock benches, ridding myself of the trauma associated with pointless exercise, I scoped out the surroundings.

The chapel is, literally, nestled in the top of a mesa; the entrance opening up to a large room filled with rows of benches, a walkway down the middle that leads to a

Ready to Write a Book?

Are you fascinated by the paranormal? Do you turn the conversation at every dinner party toward the otherwordly? Are you ready to share all the stories you've heard, and to investigate further?

We're eagerly seeking authors to pen local ghost story books. If this idea appeals to you, we'd love to hear more. Email your book idea to:

info@schifferbooks.com

or write to Acquisitions, Schiffer Publishing, Ltd. 4880 Lower Valley Rd., Atglen, PA 19310, or call 610-593-1777 to make an appointment to speak with an editor.

small landing. Sunday evening mass had already started and, highly curious, I peeked in standing just inside the doorway. At the front, massive slats of stained glass opened up to a spectacular view of Oak Creek Canyon. The sparsely decorated stone walls sloped in at an odd angle, almost A-framed, giving the church a cave-like feeling. Inside, the church seemed carefully void of any of the usual Catholic iconography. Suspicious, I wondered if there was a basement where they hid all of the scary Jesus-dying-on-the-cross stuff.

The packed congregation was standing and singing; hymnals open in their hands. A few looked up as they noticed my presence; I smiled tightly wondering if they knew that I was not one of them. They smiled back with a sincerity that felt welcoming. My anxiety eased a little and I let myself enjoy the choir of voices echoing off the stone walls.

To my left, I noticed a set of stairs that led to a bottom level. Quietly, I slipped away from the service and down the stairs so see what lay beneath. To my relief, there weren't any dungeon-themed props. However, there was a Christian-themed gift shop complete with saint key chains, prayer candles, angel statues, bookmarks with bible verses, and some tourist knick-knacks. I spotted Rudy and Gail browsing through shelves of merchandise. Rudy showed me a crown of thorns wall hanging and a tarnished wooden cross. He was considering purchasing them to aide in his daily meditation ritual. Fascinated with the iconography, he had already tattooed a rosary around his bicep. Though not Catholic, the symbolism kept him closer to faith; whereas with me it made my skin crawl in a creepy horror-movie kind of way. The Chapel of the Holy Cross had an unfamiliar comfortable feeling, though. Unfamiliar in that I didn't want to run away screaming and I was actually enjoying myself in the small underground gift shop. It emanated a peaceful feeling that put me at odds with myself because I desperately wanted to dislike the church for my own rooted issues. However, I had to resolve myself to the fact that the small church was quite possibly the most spiritual place in Sedona.

The gift shop was nearing closing, so Gail and Rudy finished up their retail transactions and we quietly headed back up the stairs, so as not to disturb the service. With their purchases in hand, we slipped out of the service while trying to be inconspicuous. Once outside, I asked Rudy if he had felt anything weird or paranormal in the church and gift shop since he had been in there longer than me and had more time to scout the place. He said that he didn't feel anything out of the ordinary, and I had to agree with him. Generally, places that felt that calm and harmonious were not ripe with paranormal activity.

Outside, I walked around the perimeter of the mesa landing to gawk at the spectacular view of the red rock mesas and buttes. From the height of where the church is situated I could see Bell Rock and the mountains where all of those poor Indians died. I shuddered at the thought. Though a beautiful aesthetic, I couldn't get the idea of carnage out of my head and it tainted the view. I went and sat down on one of the stone benches. Gail sat down with me. We eyed the massive rock structures all around us. I marveled at the beautiful hugeness of it all. In the mountain in front of us, we noticed the profile of an Indian woman and an eagle protruded from the rock. The profiles gave me the chills. There was something intentional about how the images were etched so clear in the mountain; an eerie, buzzing feeling prickled over my skin. The energy shifted and it swirled around us like a whirlpool.

Again, I saw the cave dwellers in the rocks, all around us, watching us. This time, there weren't the gruesome visions of bloodshed. They were congregating to watch us, eyeing use with intrigue. Once again I looked up at the profile of the eagle, and I realized he was a protector, a watcher of this sacred place. I believed we were on sacred ground, and what was felt on this mountain was not a vortex, but the energy of the tribe that used to call this area home. I understood the sightings of an underground civilization when meditating at the church. They were tapping into the energy source of the rock, the dead of those who dwelled there. Again, peacefulness washed over me. I felt like with every person who walked up the mountain to worship or just to see a spectacular view, they were adding to the energy of this mountain. They were healing the lost souls who died in vain. I felt like a strong part of the cycle of life and, though an epic concept, I felt like I had helped in some small way. I thanked the cave dwellers for showing themselves and telling me their story, even though it was hard to stomach.

Still, I didn't come to Sedona to have an awakening or to find grace in the small things. I came to look for haunted locations. I came to find ghosts. But what are ghosts, really? They are lost souls searching for peace. They are stuck and dysfunctional spirits looking for answers or resolutions. Unfortunately, I found the beautiful landscapes of Sedona were riddled with them — tribes of specter storytellers looming over their land.

So, are there ghosts in Sedona? You don't need to pay for a psychic to tell you the answer. You don't need fancy crystals or tours into the vortexes. You don't even have to take my word for it. Just look around and pay attention. Watch with your eyes and listen with your heart, and come to your own conclusions.

Section Three:

Jerome

JEROME

Jerome is 5,435 feet above sea level, perched on top of Mingus Mountain, which overlooks the Verde Valley. The city boasts a view that spans over fifty miles. Originally, Jerome was one of one of the rowdiest mining towns in Arizona. Today, it is an artist community with around 550 residents.

Often called the Billion Dollar Copper Camp, Jerome hosted one of the richest mines in its time. The first mining claims were filed in 1876, when Morris Andrew Ruffener found a copper deposit. After he filed the claim, Ruffener decided the deposit was too remote and non-profitable. In 1882, he sold the claim to investor Eugene Murray Jerome, a New York attorney, who started a mining company called the United Verde Copper Company. Incidentally, Jerome never visited the city for which he was named. Six years later, William A Clark purchased the United Verde Copper Company for $80,000.

Clark was considered a very modern man for his time and he helped Jerome become a successful mining town because of the amenities that he offered his mining workers. He implemented electric locomotives instead of mules in the mining tunnels and maintained strict safety requirements. Clark gave the highest pay, and supplied his workers with housing, medical care, and medical benefits that surpassed all other companies anywhere in the country. Clark made sure there was transportation into the city by financing the building of the narrow gauge railroad that had 187 curves and twenty-eight bridges in the last fourteen miles of its 27-mile run. Also, he built three swimming pools, a ballpark, and a golf course with a clubhouse for recreation.

In an eighteen-month period, from 1897-1899, Jerome suffered three catastrophic fires, which burned down most of the city. In 1899, the city was incorporated to facilitate strict building codes and establish a fire department. In 1900, the Montana Hotel opened and was called, "The finest and most ornate hostelry in Arizona Territory." However, even with the new building codes and an experienced fire department, the lavish hotel burned down in 1915. The foundation still stands today.

By 1900, Jerome was the fourth largest city in Arizona. It was known as "Ghost City," and had a terrible reputation for prostitution, opium dens, gambling, murder, and mayhem. In 1903, a headline from the *New York Sun* read, "This Jerome is a Bad One. The Arizona Copper Camp now the Wickedest Town." To remedy the prostitution issue, in 1905, the Jerome

The foundation of the Montana Hotel, which burned down in 1915.

Town Council barred women from saloons. However, in 1906, after election of a new council, the women were allowed to return. In 1909, Jerome got electricity, which was a state-of-the-art luxury for the city.

In 1918, fire once again ravaged Jerome, this time in the mines. Highly-flammable pyrite burned from depths as deep as twenty-two miles underground. One fire burned for over twenty years. Due to this, underground mining was phased out for the more convenient pit mining. However, pit mining relied on dynamite blasts, which frequently shook the city. Many buildings slid inches down the hill with every blast.

In 1935, Phelps Dodge Mining Company bought the United Verde Copper Company for $22.8 million and operated the mines until it closed down in 1953. Phelps Dodge still owns the mining rights. All together, 2.5 billion pounds of copper, 50 million ounces of silver, and 1 million pounds of gold were mined from Jerome. There are still eighty-eight miles of tunnels under the town, some reaching almost a mile down.

All of Jerome Smells Like Fire

The first thing I learned about Jerome was that Maynard James Keenan lived there. I learned this from Rudy in the back seat of the PT Cruiser as Drusilla turned left on the street that would eventually spiral us around to the top of Mingus Mountain. This time I sat on the driver's side of the car, Rudy in the middle, and Spike was on the right. Gail sat shotgun.

Maynard James Keenan is best known as the lead singer for the multi-platinum rock bands Tool and the Perfect Circle. In 2003, he started his own lesser-known side band called Puscifer.

Currently, Keenan owns three vineyards in Arizona and a produce market in Cornville. He is a self-proclaimed recluse, especially so after the birth of his child, and if you've ever seen a Tool video, you know that Keenan is on the side of eccentric. It made me wonder what kind of place Jerome was if an introverted, eclectic rocker called it home.

Being that I primarily wanted to use my psychic skills to investigate the haunted locations in Central Arizona, I didn't do much research on the cities or locations I was going to be visiting. I asked other local paranormal investigators what cities they thought would be of interest. I "Googled" the cities, made a list of places I distinctly wanted to visit, and the rest I would learn from locals telling me their experiences. I didn't check out history or look up ghost stories because I wanted to visit the locations as blind to the reports of activity as possible. It helped that I am not from Arizona and know very little about the history. In fact, I moved to Tucson on a whim, which surprised my family and friends being that I don't like dirt, cacti, or reptiles. I disliked westerns and pioneer history more than dirt, and it seemed like such an odd place to relocate. I had my personal reasons, but the for the most part, I didn't know anything about the desert except that it was hot and dirty, which was a plus from a psychic stand point because there was no way my impressions could be from some sort of unconscious memory. On the other hand, it put me at a disadvantage because I had no idea what I was getting myself into. The history of Arizona is strange, brutal, and fascinating. If nothing else, it exemplifies the strength of the human spirit.

As our carload ascended Mingus Mountain, my stomach lurched. I have a slightly annoying fear of heights. Not so bad that it paralyzes me, but just enough to make me question my sanity. The city of Jerome is literally carved into the side of the mountain and the drive up to the top was a little bit mortifying. Peering out the window there was nothing but a pretty canvas of green that dropped a few hundred feet. Though our car was fixed onto the paved road, it felt like we were suspended in mid-air, and I wondered if Zeus used Jerome as his second home away from Mount Olympus being that they were both located somewhere in the clouds.

When we reached the top of the mountain, I was not prepared for what I was about to see. Jerome was nothing like any other city I had experienced before. I had the distinct feeling I had left the modern world and had been teleported into some shoddy alternate hobbit world. I half-expected to see elves and white-bearded wizards with walking staffs wandering down the streets, except in the place of fairie folk, there were motorcycles and bikers clad in leather. A lot of bikers...

Jerome is multi-tiered; the streets are etched into the hill like platforms that are bridged together by stairways. The city reminded me of a tilted "Chutes and Ladders" board hanging precariously over the edge of a mountain. Everything about the city seemed old and frail. The streets were cracked and uneven. Sidewalks sagged and sloped. Weeds and moss invaded sidewalks. Rickety multi-floored structures slanted into the mountain like they would slide away the minute the wind started to blow. Other buildings were half-dilapidated or torn down only to their concrete foundations.

We drove across Main Street and found a parking spot near the Mile High Inn. As I got out of the car, I immediately felt claustrophobic and off-balance. There was something about the air that felt weird to me. As I breathed in, it felt thick and musty, though we were at least a mile up. It confused me because at such a high elevation the air should have been clean and crisp. I realized that it wasn't just the air that felt thick — all of Jerome felt like it had been dipped in a layer of soot. It hung over the city like a blanket. Confused, I shook the feeling off, and let curiosity get the better of me. I wanted to explore and see what sort of psychic experience Jerome had to offer. Maybe I'd run into some fairy folk and find the entrance to Middle Earth. The idea appealed to me as much as finding ghosts.

Our motley crew wandered around Main Street for awhile, admiring the old storefronts and checking out tourist traps. Inside one store, I asked a local biker with a scruffy grey beard if there were any interesting haunted locations in Jerome that I should check out. Plainly, he told me *all* of Jerome was haunted. I could walk anywhere and encounter ghosts from the past. I like that answer, but it wouldn't make for an interesting book, so I asked him if there were any specific places he had in mind. He told us we should sit a spell at the Spirit Room. It was known to be haunted.

The Spirit Room is on the corner of Main Street. It started out as the Stone Saloon in the 1880s. David Connor added to the structure when the need for a hotel arose as the mining town's population boomed. The Stone Saloon was affectionately called "Conner's Corner" because the structure burned down a total of six times and each time he took his insurance money and rebuilt in the same location.

Eventually, the Stone Saloon became an eatery called Conner's Café, which had a reputation for being one of the finest eating establishments in the territory. In 1914, John Kellner took over the café and ran it until 1919, when his lease was up. He wanted to buy the building, but David Conner's son refused to sell it to him. In the coming years, Conner's Café exchanged hands many times until 1928 when Harry Parker took over the location, including the Conner Hotel located above the café. He converted the space into a soda fountain, a Western Union office, and a bus stop. In the 1940s, the building was leased as a Mexican import and jewelry shop. When mining in Jerome was halted in the 1950s, Conner's Corner was converted to Jean's Cigar Stop, which was a popular spot for socializing. In 1961, the building changed hands again. Carrie and Rance Madonna turned the space back into a bar, calling it the Spirit Room. Though the building had been bought and sold numerous times in the last forty years, the name of the bar stayed the same.

Inside, the Spirit Room was sparsely decorated. A small painting of Jennie Banters and her scarlet women standing on a balcony of a hotel adorned the left wall. From floor to ceiling, the room was paneled with a rich, warm wood that seemed worn down by age. The dark wood bar spanned across the length of the room. Behind the bar, shelves held bottles of booze in various colors and sizes. To the left of the door, picture windows let light in the otherwise dim room. A pool table sat near the window, its green felt the only splash of color.

We sat in metal chairs at a round table near the picture of Jennie Banters. The room was almost empty save for a couple of woman bikers sitting on barstools at the bar. Rudy ordered a beer from the bar and then sat next to me. Everyone was quiet, feeling out the place. Music blared over the stereo system. The women at the bar were chatting. Nothing happened. We waited a few more minutes, watching Rudy sip on his beer. Still, nothing happened. Not an odd feeling, not a drop of weirdness in the place.

Though, I was starting to feel that sooty feeling again, like the whole building had been covered in ashes. I smelled fire in the air, and I wondered if there was a chimney nearby. I even went so far as to get up and look outside the picture windows to see where the smoke smell was coming from, but I didn't see anything that resembled smoke. I realized the curtains smelled like the pungent scent of burning wood, and I thought that to be odd.

When I sat down at the table again, Gail asked me what I was doing and wanted to know if I thought the Spirit Room was haunted. I told her, "No." I didn't think that the room had any paranormal activity. Although, I did think that the building had been on fire recently because of the smell of the red curtains in the window. The bartender came over to our table to see if Rudy wanted another beer. Since the bar seemed to be void of anything paranormal, Rudy declined and we decided to leave. But before we left, I asked the bartender if the Spirit Room had a fire anytime recently. She looked at me oddly and said, "No." There hadn't been any fire in years. I asked her, then, why did the air and the have a smell of fire. Confused, she said there wasn't a fire smell in the air, and she wasn't sure what I was talking about. I looked around my table for confirmation, and nobody smelled the fire in the air either.

The smell perplexed me. I knew that the bar wasn't haunted, but at the same time, the sense of fire was definitely coming from building. Still, when I first got out of the car I got the same sensation of soot and ashes in the air, like I was going to be choked from its heaviness. There was something obvious about Jerome that I was missing, but I wouldn't find out until later when I actually read the history.

On the other side of the street from Connor Hotel, there were steps tangled with vines and weeds that led to another street. That's how Jerome was fashioned; stairs were like bridges between the different levels of the city. You could drive around in circles or you could hoof up the steep stairways, get some unintentional exercise, and save some time.

At the first flight of stairs, there was a dirt area shrouded in shade by trees. A tall brick wall lined the back of the area creating a faux landing. Shrubbery loomed over the wall's edges. To the right, a simple mismatched playground and a set of small concrete picnic tables stuck in the dirt.

Drusilla, Rudy, and I trudged up the stairs to the landing while we waited for Spike and Gail, who were shopping. They said they were drawn to it for some reason and we should check it out to see if we got any impressions. Rudy dragged his fingers along the wall, Drusilla was drawn to a spot near the stairs, and I looked out over the landing at Main Street. The smell of fire was back, and this time, it hovered over the city like a dark cloud of brimstone and fallen ash was raining over the city. It almost felt biblical in proportion. This was getting creepy.

Drusilla's voice broke my dramatic moment. She wanted me to touch the wall to see what I felt. Distracted by the visions of the city burning to the ground, I touched the wall. Nothing...I didn't feel a thing. I asked her what she felt. She said from the wall she received a huge amount of sadness, like something horrible had happened near the wall. Rudy came over and touched the wall. He said he had the same sensation of depression or something terrible happening in the spot. I touched the wall and again all I saw was Jerome mimicking the fate of Sodom and Gomorrah. Being that I am a psychometrist, Rudy and Drusilla were rapt with attention wondering what kind of impressions I got from the wall. I shrugged my shoulders, and told them that the only thing I saw was fire. I assured them that it didn't mean their impressions were wrong. I wish I could have turned off the whole end-of-days scenery and tapped into some aspect of what happened at that wall, at least to validate their impressions. I truly believed the spot on the wall where Rudy and Drusilla felt the sadness was a trauma point for some significant event. However, we never found anything in the history pinpointing that particular spot.

In my research of Jerome, I found out that the city is notorious for burning to the ground, having done so on more than one occasion. Even though I felt slightly stupid for not figuring it out, I felt a whole lot better knowing there was a very logical conclusion to my impressions of smoke and fire. I was beginning to think that I was starting to lose my mind to some post-apocalyptic nightmare. Really, I was being true to myself and my psychic abilities, taking in the most prominent impressions first and then sorting through the rest. Only in Jerome, there were so many fires that had ravaged the city and ruined so many lives; it was hard to get past the trauma of the events to be able to interpret anything else.

From 1897-1899, fire swept through Jerome three times—and that's not counting other buildings that were afflicted with fire issues throughout its history. Fires are known to change the negative ion distribution of an environment, and there are theories to suggest that an influx of ions can cause paranormal activity. Again, everything in the paranormal world is hinged on speculation. However, after touring Jerome, I believed the scruffy biker local when he told me all of Jerome was haunted.

6

Jerome Grand Hotel

200 Hill Street, Jerome, Arizona

Directions: From Phoenix, take the I-17 Freeway and merge onto Route 260. Driving northwest to Cottonwood, turn onto Highway 89A and follow that into Jerome. Take the Prescott fork in the road and then turn onto Hill Street (which is cobblestone).

Side Note: From personal experience, Hill Street is really hard to find. It looks more like a sidewalk than a road. For reference, Hill Street is directly across from the Haunted Hamburger. If you pass it, then you've gone too far. Driving up Hill Street takes a bit of nerve and a spirit of adventure, but since you're reading a book about ghosts, I'm sure you have it in you to take it all in stride.

Reservations: For room rates and reservations, call 888-817-6788.

Website: www.jeromegrandhotel.net

Tour Times & Price: Tuesdays and Thursdays, 5 to 6:30 p.m., $20 per person. You must be a guest of the hotel to participate in the ghost tour. However, you will get a 10% discount on your reservation if you book the ghost tour and a room at the same time.

JEROME GRAND HOTEL

During the tour, you are provided with an EMF detector, an infrared thermometer, and a digital camera. A tour guide will start the tour in the boiler room and proceed to other parts of the hotel. At the end of the tour, you will be allowed to use the equipment for the rest of the night. All pictures you take will be put on a CD for you to take home.

Website: http://www.jeromeghosthunting.com/

THE HISTORY...

Built on top of Cleopatra hill, the Jerome Grand Hotel stands five stories, built in the Spanish Style that was popular in its time. It is the highest public building in Verde Valley. The structure was made of concrete poured on a fifty-degree slope, and was built to withstand blasts of up to 260,000 pounds of dynamite.

The Hotel started out as the United Verde Hospital in January 1927. By 1930, it was known as the most state-of-the-art medical facility in Arizona. The hospital closed down in 1950 due to the closing of the mines. However, it was left intact with equipment, beds, linens, and supplies in place...just in case it was needed at a later date. The hospital was never used again, and the building stayed abandoned for forty-four years. In 1970, the Phelps Dodge Mining Corporation deserted the building. It was bought, in 1994, by the Altherr family, who took two years restoring the old structure. The building has been renovated to ninety-five percent of its original state.

The Otis Elevator and Boiler Room

Installed in October 1926, the Otis Elevator at the Jerome Grand Hotel is still fully functional and services all five floors. Still in its original form, it is the oldest "self-service" elevator in Arizona. It was out-of-order for a total of four hours and fifteen minutes in the last decade, superseding most modern elevators, and travels at fifty feet per minute and takes forty-five seconds to reach the top level.

In the boiler room, the original 50-horsepower Kewanee boiler provides low-pressure steam to all of the rooms. It was considered state of the art in 1926 and still provides heat with the original General Electric pump motors.

The Ghosts...

The Jerome Grand Hotel has been called one of the most haunted locations in Arizona. Throughout its history as a hospital, many traumatic events occurred, making it a rich breeding ground for paranormal phenomenon including a hanging, a shooting, and a patient wheeling himself off the balcony to his death. The building has always been reportedly haunted.

Nurses working at the original hospital heard disembodied voices, coughing, hard breathing, moans, and cries of distress in the wards...even when there were no patients around. Doors opened and closed by themselves. Other accounts include a woman in a white dress standing out on the balcony.

Today, disembodied coughing can be heard. Fans turn on and off and guests receive phantom phone calls. Toiletries in the bathroom move or go missing. Late at night, a phantom child runs around the hallway looking for his mother.

The hotel maids have reported witnessing the smiling specter of a six-year-old boy on the third floor. Also, they have had lights turn on and off, and doors slam in front of them on their own accord. Some have complained of being pushed or disembodied voices calling out their name.

When the building was vacant, teenagers routinely explored the building, and it's said that the Otis elevator would move up and down by itself...even without electricity.

The Death Rooms

When the Jerome Grand Hotel was a hospital, there were rooms specifically used for patients who were in critical condition. These rooms were called *Death Rooms* because patients rarely lived through the night.

Now, as a hotel, the Death Rooms are still used, but have been converted into guest bedrooms, where, hopefully, its inhabitants live to check out the next morning. Many guests have said they hear a rasping sound like someone struggling for breath, or a groaning noise from someone horribly sick. Other guests have experienced blood-curdling screams.

The strangest occurrence to happen in the Death Rooms takes place when you are asleep. There are

Jerome

many accounts of guests who have had the same dream about a woman in a white outfit, presumed to be a nurse, who stands over your bed with clipboard and takes notes. What is she writing down? Is she there to make sure you make it through the night? If you dare, sleep in a Death Room and find out.

The Ghost of Mr. Harvey

Perhaps the most famous ghost of the Jerome Grand Hotel is Mr. Harvey. He was the victim of a most unfortunate murder, the specifics of which are still unsolved.

In 1935, the dead body of a hospital employee, Claude Harvey, was found at the bottom of the Otis Elevator shaft. He was the hospital's fireman engineer, known as "Scotty" to the townsmen. One morning, his body was found dead in the basement when the elevator pinned him down crushing his head. After a police investigation, it was ruled out that the elevator killed him. The body had been dumped there. Nobody knows who or why Mr. Harvey was murdered. He was a man with a good reputation and it seemed that he was well-respected in the town.

Since Mr. Harvey's grisly death, there have been many reports of paranormal activity on or near the elevator. Many have seen unexplained lights in the elevator shaft or heard the sound of creaking iron when the elevator is stopped. Some have witnessed the elevator going up and down by itself. Others have been surprised by the shadowy figure of an angry man, or felt the heavy presence of someone on the hotel stairs. Also, there have been sightings of a bearded man who has occasionally been noticed wandering around the premises. Is it the vexed spirit of Mr. Harvey stating his presence? Is he hoping someone will help him solve his murder?

7

CONNOR HOTEL

16 Main Street, Jerome, Arizona

Directions: From Phoenix, take the I-17 Freeway, merge onto Highway 260, and drive northwest to Cottonwood. Take Highway 89A into Jerome and follow it onto Hull Street...Hull Street turns into Main Street.

Reservations: For rates and reservations, call 800-523-3554.

Website: http://www.connorhotel.com/index.html

The History...

Built by David Connor in 1898, Connor Hotel was structured from rock quarried from the nearby hills, which were fired into brick in Cottonwood. At first, Connor built a one-story bar called the Stone Saloon, but as the mining in Jerome boomed, the need for a hotel became more apparent and Connor expanded the building into a hotel.

The state-of-the-art hotel housed twenty-six rooms, which were considered upscale with luxuries such as call bells, electricity, and individual wood stoves. The first floor offered a saloon with card rooms and billiard tables. The hotel even offered a bus that shuttled guests to the train depot. The price for a room was a steep $1.00 per night, which was extravagant for the time. Due to the high price of rooms, the "ladies of the night" could not afford to use the first-class establishment. Instead, there was a false storefront on the west of the building that led to "Husbands Alley."

Within the first two years of business, the Connor Hotel burnt down twice. Luckily, David Connor was one of the only two business owners in Jerome who had fire insurance. So both times, he was able to rebuild quickly, where other businesses would have been devastated by the loss.

Connor Hotel closed in 1931 when the mining in Jerome started to dwindle. The downstairs was rented out to various merchants throughout the years, though the rooms upstairs stayed empty. In the 1960s, the hotel opened again, this time as a cheap flophouse. Again, the Connor Hotel was forced to close its doors in the 1980s due to safety code issues like bad wiring and the lack of a sprinkler system. Now, the hotel is fully functional with a gift shop in its lower level.

Fire

Psychometry is the act of receiving information from an object through touch. It's an extension of my clairvoyance, which means instead of taking in energy and processing it through my "third eye" to get impressions, I touch an object and receive the information. It's sort of like "intravenous clairvoyance." The impressions are stronger and easier to sort through, and it takes a lot less concentration. Usually, I can turn the ability on and off so that I don't get impressions

1898
CONNOR
HOTEL

J
HUSBANDS' ALLEY
WITH JEROME'S ROUGH AND TUMBLE EARLY DAYS
CAME THE RED-LIGHT DISTRICT AND PROSTITUTES.
MUCH OF THE RED-LIGHT DISTRICT
WAS LOCATED ON HULL AVENUE, THE
ROAD BELOW MAIN STREET. IN 1913,
REFORMERS HELPED PASS AN ORDINANCE
RESTRICTING HOUSES OF ILL FAME FROM
BEING LOCATED DOWNTOWN. CITIZENS
SHOWED THEIR DISDAIN FOR THE LAW
BY NAMING THE ALLEYWAY FROM MAIN
STREET TO HULL AVENUE "HUSBANDS'
ALLEY". RED-LIGHT DISTRICT BUILDINGS
ON HULL AVENUE INCLUDED THE CRIBS,
A BRICK STRUCTURE THAT NO LONGER
EXISTS. THE LADIES JAIL IS STILL CURRENTLY LOCATED ON
HULL AVENUE IN THE BOTTOM FLOOR OF THE NEW STATE
MOTOR BUILDING.
FUNDED BY THE JEROME HISTORICAL SOCIETY

from everything I touch. However, sometimes I don't get a choice.

Gail and I were perusing the Connor Hotel gift shop. She was looking at cat statues and I was wandering around trying to get a feel for the place. I'm not one for baubles and postcards or other tourist paraphernalia. Don't get me wrong, I love to shop, and often find myself in a euphoric state at department store sales. However, nothing at the gift shop inspired me to take out my wallet and give up the green. Still, there were lots of pretty, lovely items to appreciate and I wandered around enjoying the leisure time. Or so I thought.

In the gift shop, there is a display case on the left side of the room. Next to it is a wooden table full of books. For the life of me I cannot remember what is in the glass case...as I was distracted by what happened next. The specifics of how I came to touch the wall of the gift shop are a little blurry to me. Later, piecing the incident together, I must have been looking at something in the case at an angle and put my hand on the wall for balance. It's the only action that makes sense since the wooden table is in the way. I guess it doesn't really matter how my hand ended up touching the wall, but in all cases my fingers grazed the butter yellow wall (or at least I remember it being yellow).

A sharp, dizzy feeling washed over me and I felt my knees nearly buckle. For a moment, I thought I was going to fall to the floor and pass out, but, luckily, I caught myself and refocused. The spinning didn't go away, but I took a breath to steady myself. There was a point where I contemplated taking my hand off the wall, but everything was happening so fast, I wasn't able to act on any realizations.

Suddenly, the room around me gave way and everything turned black. I felt like I was in some weird time loop. There wasn't a floor or a ceiling, just infinite blackness. I heard voices yelling and someone screaming. It was early morning, but the sky was still inked with night. There was a commotion outside; people congregating on the streets, hysterical. Someone was screaming again.

Fire.

There was fire all around the building. There were guests on the second floor who were not able to get to an exit because the building was already engulfed in flames. A panic-stricken man stared out a second floor window. He eyed the climbing flames with fright and horror. The man opened the window and did the only thing he could do... He jumped.

He wasn't the only one, though. There were others who had no other choice... I pulled my hand away from the wall. Stunned, I blinked a few times and looked around. I was back in the present day gift shop. I spotted Gail checking out more cat stuff. Not much had changed, and I realized I had only been in a trance for a few seconds. Disturbed by the intensity of the impression I had witnessed, I stepped outside and sat down on a bench. A mixture of sadness and grief washed over me and I took a moment to compose myself.

The Ghosts...

Many rooms at the Connor Hotel are purported to be haunted. They include:

☠ **Room 1**:The first guest in the newly renovated hotel room was the electrician. He was awakened by the sound of the whispering of a female voice. Later, he felt a cold spot in the room. Frightened, the electrician spent the rest of the night in his van. Other guests of Room 1 have experienced scratching sounds and a cold presence hovering over the bed.

☠ **Room 2**: Many guests have reported their personal articles being moved or misplaced. Plus, the furniture will move on their own accord, as well.

☠ **Room 4**: A phantom dog is believed to haunt this room. Many people have heard a dog growling, while others have cited the sound of an old man coughing.

☠ **Room 5**: Many guests have complained about electrical issues; the TV will blink on and off and clocks malfunction.

☠ Another story circulated is about a couple and their dog. The couple asked the woman at the front desk if there were any ghosts in the old hotel. Nonchalantly, the woman stated that if the couple had an open mind, then something would probably happen to them since paranormal activity was a regular occurrence. In their room, the couple experienced cold spots, the coffee pot turned on and off, and the batteries in their electrical appliances drained. Also, their dog was spooked by something and it spent the night staring at the wall. Needless to say, the couple got what they asked for, so be careful what you wish for.

8

Ghost City Inn Bed and Breakfast

541 Main Street, Jerome, Arizona

Directions: From Phoenix, take the I-17 Freeway. Merge onto the Highway 260 and drive northwest to Cottonwood. Take Highway 89A into Jerome and follow it until Hull Street; Hull Street turns into Main Street. The Ghost City Inn is on the left side.

Reservations: For room rates and reservations, call 888-634-4678.

Website: http://www.ghostcityinn.com/

GHOST
CITY
INN
BED & BREAKFAST

THE HISTORY...

Though the Ghost City Inn Bed and Breakfast has been rumored to be haunted, the name has nothing to do with its reputation. The name derives from the nickname of Jerome: "Ghost City."

The Ghost City Inn Bed and Breakfast has had many uses since it was built in the 1890s. Mainly it was used as a boarding house, lodging the copper mine middle management. Later, the Garcia family bought the building and resided in it for over thirty-five years. Briefly, the structure housed a bootleg liquor still until it blew up, damaging the second floor. In the last few years it has been a restaurant, funeral home, and an art gallery. In 1994, the structure was renovated into a bed and breakfast.

THE GHOSTS...

Throughout the bed and breakfast, there are disembodied voices and doors slam shut by themselves.

A small, older female spirit haunts the Cleopatra Room. Guests have had their cigarettes and lighters hidden from them, or they go missing. Grandma Garcia lived in the room and hated smoking and cigarettes. It is said that it is she who is misplacing the paraphernalia. Also, she has a penchant for tucking in guests when they go to bed. Guests have felt the presence of an older woman hovering over their bed, pushing the covers in around them.

In the Northern Exposure Room, guests have been rudely awakened by a spirit touching their face and pulling down the covers.

A gray figure dressed in a long duster shows himself in the Verde Room. The apparition is presumed to be a cowboy, though he has long gray hair and is not wearing a hat. The cowboy appears between the hours of 2:30 a.m. and 2:30 p.m. What happened in those twelve hours? Were those the hours he worked at the mine? Is the cowboy trying to convey his time of death?

9

The Mile High Grille & Inn

309 Main Street, Jerome, Arizona

Directions: From Phoenix, take I-17 and merge onto Highway 260. Drive northwest to Cottonwood. Take Highway 89A into Jerome and follow it onto Hull Street; Hull Street will turn into Main Street.

Reservations: For rates, reservations, and hours of operation, call 928-634-5094

Website: http://www.jeromemilehighinn.com/

The History...

Known as the Clinksdale Building, the Mile High Inn, built in 1899, was formerly the Inn at Jerome. The original structure had burned down. The new building was rebuilt with brick walls eighteen inches thick to make it as fireproof as possible.

The Mile High Inn became a popular bordello run by the notorious Madam Jennie Banters...until city officials tried to appropriate a new, more "civilized" reputation, forcing the "soiled doves" into a more private, less conspicuous street they dubbed "Husbands Alley."

When the bordello moved, the Mile High Inn's clientele dwindled. Eventually the building became a hardware store, with the rooms rented out as apartments. The building housed a myriad of other businesses until it was reformed back into an inn with a restaurant on the ground level.

The Ghosts...

- A spectral cat that leaves phantom paw prints on the beds and brushes up against the legs of unsuspecting guests, especially in the restaurant;
- Radios turning on and off;
- Whistling and disembodied voices heard throughout the building;
- A cherub statue in the restaurant that turns around on its own accord;
- Glasses sliding off tables, crashing to the floor;
- Electrical appliances that seem to have a mind of their own, randomly turning on and off.

☠ A shadowy male figure with a disapproving look on his face lurking in the Victoria Room, as well as the restaurant. This grumpy male sweeps through the room like an eerie cold breeze, chilling guests to the bone. Other guests have described smells of an old perfume and hair-perming solution.

☠ A maid threatened by a vase that flew straight in the air at her, crashing against the wall. Later, another vase was placed in the same spot...it also flew through the air and crashed to the floor.

☠ The ghost of an older man freely roams the Pillow Talk and Kiss and Tell rooms. He is described as wearing a felt hat, a long-sleeved work shirt, suspenders, and work pants tucked into knee-high boots. Being a mischievous ghost, he is often blamed for leaving depressions on the newly made beds. He seems to object to the paintings in the Kiss and Tell Room, taking them off the wall and putting them into the armoire. The armoire often opens and closes by itself.

☠ In the Memories of the Heart Room, a couple awoke from light pouring into the room. They realized their door had opened by itself, but when they arose from bed to close the door, they were surprised to watch it silently close again. They got up to check the door; mysteriously the door was completely shut and even the deadbolt lock had been turned.

The Ghost of Madam Jennie Banters

Madam Jennie Banters was said to be the richest woman in Northern America, making a handsome living entertaining men with drink and sex. She started her career at the Mile High Inn, which became a popular attraction for the mining workers who desired entertainment and leisure after their grueling workweek stuck in the mines. When Jerome tried to reform its image, Jennie's bordello was forced into "Husband's Alley," along with the other scarlet women. Shortly after her move, Jennie was allegedly murdered by one of her male clients.

Soon after renovations of the Mile High Inn were completed, Jennie's ghost became a staple sighting, especially in the restaurant where she liked to move utensils around, even tossing an ice cream scoop to the ground. Cookbooks have been reported to slide across the counters until they hit the floor. Jennie has no problem showing herself as an apparition. Sometimes she is seen with her favorite cat keeping pace at her side. Owners surmised that she was not entirely happy with the changes of the building and had been keeping watch over the renovations.

Also, Jennie is fond of the Lace and Lariat Room. She'll rearrange the furniture and plays with the ceiling fan. Objects are moved and left in odd places, much to the annoyance of maids and confused guests.

10

The Haunted Hamburger

410 North Clark Street, Jerome, Arizona

Directions: From Phoenix, drive the I-17 Freeway North. Take Highway 260 northwest toward Cottonwood and turn onto Highway 89A. Follow it into Jerome to Hull Street. From Hull Street turn right to Main Street. Main Street turns into Clark Street. The Haunted Hamburger is on the right. *(Hull Street, Main Street, and Clark Street all circle around each other. So, if you miss it the first time drive around in a loop and come back to it.)* For their hours, call 928-634-0554.

JEROME PALACE
THE HAUNTED HAMBURGER
BURGERS
CHICKEN
SALADS
CHEESE STEAKS
FIRE EXIT

Originally, the Haunted Hamburger was supposed to be a Mexican restaurant, but the owners changed their minds shortly before opening day. Contractors who renovated the three-story building, which used to be the Wykoff Apartments in the 1920s, experienced a series of paranormal events, including disappearing tools and ladders, slamming doors, flickering lights, and water faucets that turned on and off of their own accord.

Working in an actively haunted environment, the contractors nicknamed the building "that haunted hamburger joint." The name stuck, and the rest, as they say, is history.

11

Other Jerome Ghost Spots & Stories

Husbands Alley & the Crib District

Prostitution was a common trade in Jerome, giving the mining city a terrible reputation. In 1913, as an act to clean up the city, reformers outlawed houses of ill repute from the downtown area. Many bordellos relocated to Hull Avenue, a street that could be accessed by an alleyway from Main Street, where they originally resided. They called it "Husbands Alley" as a way to protest the law.

Prostitution thrived in the new Crib District — it was estimated that over one hundred prostitutes lived in Jerome. The prettiest girls worked in the more respectable brothels, which were run by madams. Other women rented shacks along the alley that were simply referred to as "cribs."

Nora Brown is credited as being the first madam in Jerome. Though not thought of as an attractive woman, Nora had a good head for business and had a reputation

This walkway at the edge of the Connor Hotel used to be called "Husbands Alley." At the other end is Hull Avenue that housed the Crib District.

for being able to hold her liquor as good as any man. She had a jovial disposition and a horse-like laugh. The story goes that Madam Brown introduced Jennie Banters to the lifestyle that would make her an infamous part of Jerome's history.

When walking down the Crib District, tourists have claimed to hear the catcalls of the "soiled doves" luring them into their cribs. Others have experienced a presence watching them or dark shadows silently moving in the periphery. The smell of old perfume lingers in the air.

Sammie Dean, a popular prostitute, was strangled in the Crib District by one of her clients. The mystery of who murdered her is still unsolved today. Some say her spirit wanders down the street hoping someone will hear her pleas and, eventually, solve her death.

Jerome Community Center

Formerly known as Lawrence Memorial Hall, the Jerome Community Center is now known affectionately as "Spook Hall." Before its respectable stint as the J. C. Penny building, the area was better known for housing the cribs where the "ladies of the night" provided their services.

Unfortunately, prostitution was a dangerous business, and one woman was the victim of a grisly crime. Stabbed by a miner, her body was left on the street. Her silhouette is seen in front of Spook Hall, where she lingers, and then walks down the street toward a hotel and suddenly vanishes.

What is left of the Crib District.

Phelps Dodge Mine

A miner nicknamed "Headless Charlie" was decapitated in the mines. His body was found, but not his head. Shortly after his death, workers found large footprints in the mine while others heard disembodied footsteps and encountered a shadowy figure. It is said that Headless Charlie lurks in the old mines looking for his lost head.

The Clinic

Just below the Jerome Grand Hotel there is an abandoned building that used to be a clinic that housed the patients from the 1917 influenza epidemic, all of whom inevitably died. It is said that during full moons, the ghosts of former patients can be seen in the windows.

The Wailing Woman

Locals tell a horrific tale of a woman who drowned her children in a nearby river. The woman was mother to three small children, all under the age of five. Her husband was killed in a mining accident, and the woman was left with a family to support and no way to make money.

One night the woman walked her children down to the river after it had rained. The river was swollen with water and flowing heavily downstream. In her grief, she threw the children in the river, one by one. Each child thrashed and cried out to their mother as they were whisked away by the river's intense current. Intent on her task, she showed no remorse and went home.

The next morning, when her head cleared, the woman realized the horrific deed she had committed. Hysterical, she ran down the river, hoping, miraculously, that her children had survived the rushing river. Unfortunately, the mother found the dead bodies of her three children downstream. Heartbroken, she lamented over her children, and threw herself in the river to drown alongside them.

Today, locals say that after the rains, you can hear the wailing of the woman as she cries for her children. Some have seen the silhouette of a crying woman bending over the river.

Jerome Cemetery

Locals tell a frightening tale of a phantom dog with red glowing eyes that resides in the cemetery. The dog doesn't like to be disturbed and, if spotted, he will chase you out of the cemetery. Other paranormal activity includes disembodied footsteps, unexplained voices, and dark shadows.

We Are Not Alone

The Jerome Cemetery was hard to find and a bit of a challenge. The turn that you must take to get to the small cemetery looked more like a drop-off over a cliff than an actual road. But as paranormal investigators we are sometimes too numb to the sense of danger, and with butterflies in our stomach, we surged forward over the steep hill. With relief, we found a cramped, beaten path that led to a haphazard cemetery at the edge of a sloping cliff. Stacy parked the Durango at a rusty gate. Markus and Kendra decided not to go into the cemetery because of their own personal beliefs, but Stacy and I couldn't wait to snoop around and walked around the gate.

The cemetery was old and dilapidated. Crumbling headstones slanted at an angle, their bases uprooted from the years of the shifting hill sliding down the

cliff. While Stacy took pictures, I meandered around feeling out the site. The cemetery definitely had a buzzing feeling associated with a haunted location. It felt like a tingling sensation all over my body. I heard what seemed like a thousand voices whispering in my ear. It was the typical sensation I encountered in a haunted cemetery, like the dead were all eager to talk to someone who could hear them. The sensations were beginning to make me feel uncomfortable and I couldn't focus on just one voice. My mediumship abilities are not as strong as my other psychic skills, so I decided to head back to the car. Stacy lingered to take a few more pictures.

When I reached the Durango, Kendra asked me if I felt something. I told her that I felt like there was more than one spirit and that we definitely *weren't* alone. At that moment, I heard Stacy yell my name. I turned and she was hustling toward me with an anxious look on her face. As she got closer, she told us she heard the distinct sounds of footsteps behind her. Then she felt the strong presence of someone. It scared her, so she walked away fast as she could.

Section Four:

COTTONWOOD

f-stop
Tour Bus
Parking

Named after the massive trees that line the Verde River, Cottonwood is a small, relaxed community situated in the heart of the Verde Valley, between Prescott and Sedona. It's also surrounded by the rugged mountains of Yavapai County. To the north there is a spectacular view of the red rock mesas and buttes of Sedona landscape. In the historic Old Town of Cottonwood, the wild peacock population is encouraged to roam freely down the streets. The high sidewalks and false fronts give the city an "old time" feeling.

Like much of Verde Valley, the first inhabitants of the land were Native Americans, notably the Sinagua, and then later the Apache and Yavapai tribes. The first Anglo pioneers did not settle in the area until the 1870s.

Charles D. Willard founded Cottonwood in 1879. He named the settlement after sixteen Cottonwood trees that lined the Verde River a quarter-mile away. Mosquitoes plagued the area from the stagnant pools of water left by flooding, and Malaria and dysentery afflicted many settlers, becoming a severe health problem. Quinine was sold for $4.00 an ounce (when in surplus from Camp Verde) to alleviate the diseases.

Despite the health problems, Cottonwood flourished. Most pioneers farmed and raised cattle; they grew vegetable crops and grains to sell to the soldiers at Camp Verde and eventually the Jerome population. Their main source of meat came from the rabbit and quail that populated in the overgrown native grasses.

Cottonwood was known for its lawlessness. While other cities like Jerome were continually trying to amend their image, Cottonwood seemed to be overlooked by the eyes of scrutiny. The town soon had a reputation for its heavy bootlegging trade, boasting the best bootleg booze in the West. Many traveled from as far as Los Angeles for a taste of Cottonwood hooch.

Besides its illegal trade, the city was a thriving place for businessmen and merchants. Many settlers from surrounding cities bought their goods from Cottonwood, making it a town with more businesses per capita than any other in Arizona. By the 1920s, Cottonwood was called, "The Biggest Little Town in Arizona." The city was incorporated in 1960, and many improvements were made, especially to the streets and highways. Now, Cottonwood is still a haven for shopping and sightseeing.

12

COTTONWOOD HOTEL

930 North Main Street, Cottonwood, Arizona

Directions: From Phoenix, take I-17 and get off at the Camp Verde Exit (287). Turn left at Highway 260 (towards Cottonwood). Drive Highway 260 to Highway 89A (toward South Main Street). Stay on Highway 89A for three miles (South Main Street will turn into North Main Street) and drive into Historic Old Town Cottonwood. The hotel will be on your left.

Reservations: For rates and Reservations, call 928-634-9455

Website: www.cottonwoodhotel.com/home.html

MAIN ST
PINAL

The History...

Considered the longest standing building in Cottonwood, Antonio and Mary Giordano first built the Cottonwood Hotel in 1922. The downstairs was a clothing store and the upstairs the hotel. In the 1930s, the Giordanos died and their daughter Catherine took over the business with her husband Bill Robinson. Until the 1980s, the building stayed in the Giordano family.

In 1925, Cottonwood experienced the biggest catastrophe in its history. A still located at the Thomas Moore Restaurant exploded. Winds fanned the flames of the vicious fire across two blocks of the west side of Main Street. Fifteen business buildings were ravished in the fires as well as ten residences. Even though nearly half of the city was burned to the ground, there was only one casualty.

The Cottonwood Hotel was rebuilt exactly to its original plans except for an addition of a balcony. Due to new fire insurance regulations, the new building was built from solid cast concrete block with twelve to eighteen inches of firewall. Ironically, after the Cottonwood Hotel was rebuilt, the town fire bell was put on the roof of the Cottonwood Hotel. The fire chief rang it until a fire department was put together.

In the 1940s, the Robinsons added to the hotel to extend their living space. The addition can be seen in the movie "Desert Fury," starring Burt Lancaster and Lizabeth Scott. Many other famous people stayed in the Cottonwood hotel including Mae West and John Wayne. Even Elvis Presley visited Cottonwood while he filmed "Stay Away, Joe."

Presently, Karen Leff owns the hotel and has renovated it nearly to its original specifications. A self-proclaimed historian of Cottonwood, Leff has carefully researched the hotel history, which is displayed on the website. The five long-term-stay suites are named after notable characters in its past: George H. Brooks, Mae West, Desert Fury, Elvis, and John Wayne.

Hollywood Beckons...

A Frequent Visitor

Known for her bawdy double entendres, Mae West was a big-mouthed sex symbol during the turn of the century. She made a name for herself in Vaudeville, and later as a writer and actress in Hollywood pictures. In the 1920s, Mae West roomed at Cottonwood Hotel and she frequented the backrooms of the city's infamous speakeasies. Old timers tell stories of West in the back alleys running her hands through the mash in the whisky barrels that would become hooch. Later she stayed at the hotel in the 1930s on her way back to Los Angeles from her New York stage show. The Cottonwood Hotel has an upstairs room called the Mae West Suite in honor of her visits to the hotel.

Considered a threat to morality, Mae West was constantly under scrutiny because of her sexy, independent demeanor and her racy quips. She wrote, produced, and directed her own plays, the most popular called "*Sex*," which was a hit on Broadway. Though reviews of the risqué play were poor, ticket sales were favorable. This, however, was not enough to keep city officials from raiding the production and incarcerating Mae West on Welfare Island for "corrupting the morals of youth." She only ended up serving eight days of her ten-day sentence, receiving two days off for good behavior.

Jail time didn't seem to faze Mae West, who wrote many other plays that put a light on controversial subjects like homosexuality and transgender. Her notoriety shot her into fame, and in 1932, Paramount Pictures offered her a film contract. West was offered a minor role in "Night After Night" starring George Raft. Reportedly, she was not happy with her dialogue and only agreed to be in the picture if she would be allowed to rewrite her part.

She wrote bawdy one-liners that would fuel her career with fame and notoriety. For instance, in "Night After Night," a hatcheck girl said to West, "Goodness, what lovely diamonds," referring to a sparkling necklace around her neck.

West replied, "Goodness has nothing to do with it, dearie."

Mae West became an instant movie star, and George Raft is quoted as saying, "She stole everything but the cameras."

Her next film, "She Done Him Wrong," starred a relatively unknown actor named Cary Grant. He was nominated for an Academy Award, which ignited his career and is said to have saved Paramount Pictures from going bankrupt. Following "She Done Him Wrong" was another movie with Cary Grant that was a huge blockbuster of its time. By 1935, West was the second highest paid person in the United States, second only to William Randolph Hearst. However, conservatives were up in arms about West's steamy scenes and overt sexuality.

In 1934, a series of censorship guidelines were put together nicknamed, the Production Code. West's films were scrutinized heavily under these guidelines, but it did not stop her. Instead, she wrote more sexy quips into her films, hoping the censors would edit the obvious ones, leaving the more subtle one-liners in the production. In the next ten years, Mae West made a slew of popular movies until 1943 when the film "The Heats On" bombed at the box office. She went back to Broadway and later starred in her own one-man-show in Las Vegas. At the age of 60, Mae West was offered the role of Norma Desmond in "Sunset Boulevard." She turned it down because she believed she was too sexy for the role.

Toward the end of her career, West wrote a best-selling autobiography, recorded two rock-n-roll albums, and made a number of guest appearances on television.

In 1980, Mae West suffered a stroke. While in the hospital, she had a diabetic reaction to her feeding tube and had another stroke. Paralyzed on her right side, she caught pneumonia. In November, after recuperating, West was sent home. She died at the age of 87. Her star is on the Hollywood Walk of Fame at 1560 Vine Street in Hollywood California.

Romance at Cottonwood Hotel

John Wayne is an icon in American cinema. In 1999, he was named thirteenth on the list of "Greatest Male Stars of All Time" from the American Film Institute. Wayne is known for being the embodiment for true rugged masculinity, starring as the moral protagonist in over one hundred films. He won an Academy Award for "True Grit" in 1970.

As a teenager, Gail Russell was scouted by Paramount Pictures because of her beauty. She had an extremely introverted personality and was insecure about acting, but Paramount believed she had great promise and assigned her an acting coach. Gail made her first film, "Henry Aldrich Gets Glamour," at the age of 19.

Her most notable picture was "The Invited" that, ironically, was the beginning of her addiction to alcohol and her inevitable demise. Russell had terrible stage fright and drank to ease her nerves. The drinking took over and in July 1957 she drove her car through the front of Jan's Coffee Shop. A picture of her drunk and sitting in the rubble of her car was plastered on the front page of the *L.A. Times*. After the incident, Russell did two more movies. Unfortunately, Gail Russell was found in dead in her Brentwood apartment. She had a heart attack that was attributed to alcoholism and malnutrition. She was only thirty-six years old.

John Wayne and Gail Russell starred in two films together. Their alleged affair caused quite a scandal in Hollywood and was scrutinized in a tumultuous divorce between John Wayne and his second wife, Esperanza Baur.

John Wayne met Baur in Mexico City in 1941 while he was still married to his first wife, Josephine Saenz. Baur was a foreign actress who starred in a variety of Spanish-speaking films. In December 1945, Wayne divorced Saenz, and, shortly after, in January 1946, he married Baur. Their relationship was turbulent from the start. Baur was jealous of Wayne's dedication to his career and his four children from the previous marriage. They continually argued and there were rumors of physical altercations.

In 1946, John Wayne and Gail Russell starred in the first of two movies. Their first film, "Angel & the Bad Man," was filmed in Sedona, but for the "rushes" the cast and crew used the Rialto Theater in Cottonwood for its convenience. Rushes were private screenings of the film dailies where the cast and crew reviewed and edited their progress.

It is reported that after the rushes, Wayne and Russell did not return to Sedona. Instead they checked into the Cottonwood Hotel on a few occasions for a secret rendezvous. Locals have reported witnessing Wayne and Russell kissing in the doorway of their room, and holding hands and kissing each other between the racks in the Robinson's clothing store downstairs.

At the wrap of the filming of "Angel & the Bad Man," the cast and crew were thrown a party. Wayne came home late to a drunk and enraged Baur, who accused him of having an affair with his beautiful costar. Baur pulled a gun on Wayne and tried to shoot him as he attempted to walk through the front door.

The turbulent couple stayed together almost seven years, separating in 1952. The divorce hearings in 1953 were vicious, and there were charges of infidelity, spousal abuse, drunken violence, and emotional cruelty. Wayne accused Baur of having an affair with hotel heir, Nicky Hilton.

Again, Baur accused Wayne of having an affair with Russell. Both Russell and Wayne vehemently denied they were ever intimate with each other. Still, the proceedings stressed an already shaky marriage with her husband, Guy Madison, who was a character actor for RKO. A year later, Russell and Madison also divorced. In 1955, Esperanza Baur died of a heart attack.

To commemorate John Wayne's stay, the Cottonwood Hotel has a suite named after him

The Ghosts...

At Cottonwood Hotel, the paranormal activity includes unexplained footsteps in the upstairs hallway. Pictures on the walls are turned upside down or dropped to the floor. Many have complained about their "loud neighbors" after hearing the sound of furniture being dragged around, thuds, and loud noises...only later learning that the suite had been empty their entire stay. A couple in another suite reported hearing noises in the "Desert Fury" Room. They described hearing a door opening and closing, the bed squeaking, and the shower turning on and off. Later, from Leff, they found out they had been the only inhabitants of the building.

The Ghost of George H. Brooks

Perhaps the most eerie ghost story told about the Cottonwood Hotel is about spiritualist and psychic, Minister George Brooks. Brooks was a Doctor of Divinity, and routinely traveled the country speaking on Metaphysics. He was born in London England, but moved to Los Angeles, California, with his wife and son in the 1920s.

Brooks visited Cottonwood Hotel almost monthly, hosting seminars and lectures in Cottonwood and Sedona. He was said to be a warm, straightforward man with a keen sense of humor. Even though most of the townspeople strayed from him because of his psychic predictions, he had a way with the children, entertaining them with stories about his travel.

In 1925, Brooks predicted that Cottonwood would see its biggest catastrophe. On the night after his prediction, a bootlegging still blew up on the west side of Cottonwood, burning down the hotel and fifteen other business buildings. Ironically, Brooks was the one and only fatality. His skeletal remains were found in the burnt rubble. He was half-clothed at the foot of the bed. Some surmised Brooks was putting his clothes on to escape, but passed out from smoke inhalation. Others believed he might have been murdered because of his metaphysical beliefs.

When recent owner Karen Leff first renovated the hotel in 1996, she found strange images on the walls in Unit 3, now called the George H. Brooks Suite. A few years later, she learned about the mysterious death of George Brooks from his great-great-granddaughter. Leff was given a picture of Brooks. She compared it to the pictures of the strange images on the walls—there seemed to be an uncanny resemblance. Are the spectral footsteps in the upstairs hallway those of George trying to find a way out of his burning room? Did George etch his ghostly image into the wall of Unit 3? You can view the pictures of George Brooks and the phantom images on the hotel's website to decide for yourself.

Disappearing Ghosts

I walked down the street of Historic Old Town Cottonwood searching for the hotel. I found it on the corner of Main and Pinal streets and looked, unsuccessfully, for a lobby. From a flyer at what seemed like the front entrance, the hotel mostly caters to extended-stays and I assumed there was no need for a receptionist. On the paper there was the name Karen Leff and a phone number. She was the owner and the person you spoke to for reservations or inquiries. I was writing the information down in my notebook as Rudy came around the corner. He asked me what I was doing. I told him that the Cottonwood Hotel was supposedly haunted.

As we talked at the front of the hotel, a woman passed by and asked if we needed any help. I told her I was writing a book about hauntings in the area and I was looking for the owner of the hotel. She stated she *was* Karen Leff, the owner.

While standing in front of the hotel, I asked her about the haunted history of the building. Karen told me that when she first renovated the structure, she had some strange things happen to her—the most notable being the weird images she found on the walls of Unit 3 that seemed to resemble the picture of George Brooks. Shortly after the incident, she had the hotel exorcised and blessed. Since then, she has had no problems with paranormal activity. According to Leff, the hotel is no longer haunted.

Is it really that easy to get rid of a ghost? Is the specter of George Brooks merely lying dormant or has he really been exorcised? Visit Cottonwood Hotel and come to your own conclusions.

Section Five:

Flagstaff

Flagstaff

Flagstaff sits at the base of a dormant volcano part of the San Francisco Peaks. The city is home to Lowell Observatory and the Museum of Northern Arizona, one of the most comprehensive archeological museums of the prehistoric southwest in the world. There are many versions of how Flagstaff became a territory, but there is one thing that stays the same—there was a literal flagstaff involved.

In 1871, Edward Ripple settled in the area and built a saloon. The second pioneer would not come for another five years. His name was F. F. McMillen and he laid claim near Antelope Spring. A few months later, a scouting party from Boston camped near the spring. The area was an open valley with very little shrubbery except for one lone pine tree. In some versions of the story, it was 1876 around Independence Day. In other accounts, it was sometime in May. In either case, the scouting party stripped away the branches of the tree, placed a hoop at the top, and ran an American flag up the pine. Soon, the scouting party headed west, leaving their "flag staff" for other pioneers to use as a landmark and the name stuck.

At first the Flagstaff area was desolate, only housing a few settlers and a handful of sheepherders who used the flatlands for their livestock. That soon changed with the emergence of the railroad. In 1880, the Atlantic and Pacific Railroad began laying track down in Albuquerque and westward to California. Pioneers took advantage of the new crop of train workers, selling them food, provisions, and entertainment from supply camps they set up along the railroad trail.

Soon a settlement began to form on Mars Hill just outside of present day Flagstaff; it was mostly comprised of saloons, gambling houses, and dance halls. Businesses thrived catering to the transient train workers who migrated through the area. By 1882, the railroad had been finished and the population dwindled. Still many entrepreneurs and pioneers stayed, hoping the new railroad would bring travelers who would, in turn, bring in business to the small settlement. In time, Flagstaff became a consistent stop for water and servicing of the trains as they passed through on their way to California. More sheep and cattle ranchers migrated to Flagstaff because the inexpensive flatlands were perfect for grazing livestock. With the convenience of the train, they realized it was affordable to transport their beef to the Eastern market. Other businessmen took advantage of the train, including E. E. Ayers, who setup the largest mill in Flagstaff and used the transportation to ship lumber throughout the United States. Within months, the town boomed with a thriving lumber and livestock industry, and merchants who provided hotels, saloons, and cafés to weary travelers and cowboys.

Old Town, New Town

In 1883, the train depot in Flagstaff moved about a half-mile outside of the town so that the trains did not have to start their engines up a steep hill. Entrepreneur J. P. Brannen saw the move as an opportunity and moved his business across the street from the depot. Others followed suit, building on what became known as Front Street. Flagstaff became two settlements: Old Town, where the depot used to be situated, and New Town, where it moved. In 1884, a fire ravished Old Town, and New Town became the only settlement and is where Flagstaff is situated today.

Though New Town had mercantile, Old Town had water. After a series of fires devastated the old settlement, the issue of how water would be transported into New Town became of great concern. Logical conclusions led to the idea of tapping into the San Francisco Springs, but the costs far outweighed the feasible means of a small settlement like Flagstaff. City officials proposed incorporating to gain status, but, more importantly, to afford the opportunity of selling municipal bonds to pay for the water project. In 1894, a petition was circulated among the townspeople and in May Flagstaff became an incorporated town.

Today, Flagstaff is a tourist gateway to the Grand Canyon. The lush pinewood forests and rugged terrain of the desert are ideal for outdoor hobbies like hiking, horseback riding, and skiing. The historic Route 66 runs through downtown.

13

WEATHERFORD HOTEL

23 North Leroux, Flagstaff, Arizona

Directions: From Phoenix, take I-17 North. As you enter Flagstaff, the I-17 Freeway turns into Milton Road, which will become Route 66. Continue on Route 66 to Leroux Street and turn left. Go one block. The hotel will be on your left.

Reservations: For rates and reservations, call 928-779-1919.

Website: http://www.weatherfordhotel.com/

The History

Texas-born deputy John Weatherford initially rode into Flagstaff to dispel the rumors spreading about the notorious Graham-Tewkesbury feud, which would be immortalized in Zane Grey's novel, *To the Last Man*.

The Grahams were cattlemen and the Tewkesbury family herded sheep. Their dispute revolved around land and water boundaries that escalated over the years. It was no secret that the two clans disliked each other, but the animosity turned deadly, lasting ten years and claiming over twenty lives.

In 1887, the feud escalated when Tom Graham ambushed a Tewkesbury employee near the Mogollon Rim, which was the established border between their two lands. Later, the Grahams surrounded the Tewkesbury residence in the early morning shooting down John Tewkesbury as he walked out of his house. A gun battle commenced for hours and, in the chaos, a herd of hogs escaped from their pen. They feasted on the dead body of John Tewkesbury until his wife walked out of the house with a shovel and began to bury him in the very place he laid. Even though no truce was announced, the Grahams backed down in respect to the grieving woman.

The last killing cited between the two families was in 1892. There were trials, and guilty parties who had gotten involved in the feud were hanged. It was around this time that John Weatherford came into town to set straight the rumors that were flying around about the Graham-Tewkesbury dealings.

In 1896, Weatherford decided to build the first hotel in Flagstaff on the corner of Leroux Street and Aspen Avenue. Weatherford was granted permission to build the hotel in 1898 as long as he abided by new city ordinances that stated the structure be constructed from brick or stone to prevent fire damage. Also, he was instructed to construct a sidewalk along Leroux Street and Aspen Avenue to improve the area. Sidewalks were not typical at the time; unpaved walkways were dusty during the summer, muddy during the rains and winter.

Construction commenced and, on January 1, 1900, Weatherford Hotel opened to the public. The hotel was three stories and held forty-two rooms. It was said to be the finest and most luxurious hotel in the entire Southwest.

Many celebrities stayed at the Weatherford, including President Franklin D. Roosevelt, newspaper mogul William Randolph Hearst, and infamous lawman Wyatt Earp. Novelist Zane Grey wrote his book, *The Call of the Canyon,* while residing at the hotel.

On January 31, 1872, Pearl Zane Grey was born in Zanesville, Ohio. As a child he got into many violent alterations and his father tried to curb his anti-social behavior by severely beating him. Due to this, his relationship with his father was strained. However, he forged a loving relationship with his mother and a father substitute named Muddy Miser. The old man approved of Grey's love of reading, fishing, and writing and supported him in the pursuit of becoming a writer, an unconventional lifestyle for the time. At fifteen, Grey wrote his first short story called "Jim in the Cave." When his father found the story, he tore it to pieces and beat him.

In 1889, Grey's father invested badly and moved the family to Columbus to spare them from embarrassment. He tried reestablishing his dental business in the new city and employed Grey as an assistant. Grey helped by making rural house calls and performing extractions. He practiced basic dentistry until the state board stopped him.

Grey played baseball during the summers and was scouted by an agent. He received offers from many colleges and finally decided on the University of Pennsylvania. Grey struggled with the idea of becoming a writer, but decided to study dentistry like his father because it would be more practical. Though an average student, Grey excelled in baseball as a pitcher and played baseball throughout his college years. He had the opportunity to play in the minor leagues, but decided to start a dentistry practice in New York instead. It was a competitive area, but Grey wanted to be close to publishers so that he could try his hand at writing to ease the tedium of dentistry. The love of writing never truly left his blood.

In 1905, Grey married Lina "Dolly" Roth. The pair had an intense five-year courtship full of passion and arguments. Grey was prone to mood swings and had a wandering eye that added stress to their already tumultuous relationship. However, the couple loved each other and Dolly turned a blind-eye to his discretions. She thought of his mistresses as a weakness rather than a betrayal of their relationship.

Dolly studied to become a schoolteacher, but abandoned the idea after marriage. She came from money and was allotted an inheritance and dedicated herself to the family and supporting Grey in his writing. Grey quit his dentistry practice and wrote full time. Dolly managed his writing career, taking half of the proceeds. The married couple had three children together and she used her part of the money to take care of the family household.

With Dolly's educational background, she aided Grey by editing his works and improving his writing style. In 1903, Harper Collins rejected his first novel, *Betty Zane*. Dejected, he decided to self-publish the book. Throughout the years, Grey traveled in the wilderness, taking hunting and camping trips. He took copious descriptions of the landscape and his personal conversations, using them as inspirations for his novels. Grey wrote about his adventures in the treacherous wilderness, however, Harper Collins did not feel that his writing was worthy and rejected his next three books.

With his first child on the way, Grey felt an urgency to produce a viable novel that would become published. He tried his hand at a western and produced it in four months. In 1910, *Heritage of the Desert* was accepted by Ripley Hitchcock, editor of Harper Collins, and became a best seller. Grey stuck to the western genre, producing a slew of best-selling novels including his most famous, *Riders of the Purple Sage*, which was later turned into a feature film. With the success of the movie, there was a large interest in his other works, and many were adapted for the silver screen. The character in his novel, The *Lone Star Ranger*, became the inspiration for the popular TV show, "The Lone Ranger." To capitalize on his success, Grey started his own production company. He became one of the first millionaire writers of the time.

The money gave Grey leisure time to travel extensively and engage in his favorite past time: fishing. Though his home base was in Altadena, California, he spent much time in Central Arizona and Flagstaff. He had a cabin near the Mogollon Rim where he would spend time relaxing. The quiet time away seemed to ease his nerves and lessen his bouts of depression. He spent most of his later years traveling to remote locations, including Australia and New Zealand. In October 1939, Zane Grey died at his home in Altadena of heart failure.

In the 1930s, the Weatherford Hotel business declined and the building housed a variety of other businesses including the first telephone exchange company, a few restaurants, a theatre, a tavern, and a billiard hall. Since the 1970s, the hotel has been owned by Henry Taylor and Pamela Green, who restored it. It's been a working hotel for the past thirty years.

THE GHOSTS...

The Zane Grey Ballroom seems to be the hub of paranormal activity in the Weatherford Hotel. The second-floor room is surrounded by stain glass windows and opens up to a double-tiered balcony. A lady in white has been spotted on numerous occasions floating across the hardwood floor. Sometimes the woman is merely seen on one side of the room...only to dart across the other side with inhuman speed.

Guests have reported that the light over the pool table sways by itself, or they hear whispers at the bar in an otherwise empty room.

The most popular ghosts at the Weatherford stem from a chilling tale of love and murder. In the 1930s, a couple was brutally killed in Room 54 on their wedding day. An employee who was staying in the room woke up in the middle of the night. She witnessed the specter couple sitting at her foot of her bed. Now the room has been converted to a storage closet, but guests and staff still report sightings of a couple in the area.

On the fourth floor, housekeeping have reported hearing their name being called by a disembodied voice or witnessing a presence standing behind them near the stairs. The basement is also said to have a cold spot and a very weird sinister feeling.

14

Hotel Monte Vista

100 North San Francisco Street, Flagstaff, Arizona

Directions: Take the I-40 Freeway, following the signs to Highway 89 (Milton Road). Turn left on San Francisco Street. The hotel is on the right.

Reservations: For rates and reservations, call 800-545-3068.

Website: http://www.hotelmontevista.com/

THE HISTORY...

In the 1920s, tourism boomed in Flagstaff, leaving the city with a need for first-class accommodations for travelers coming in by train. Most of the hotels in the area were out-modeled for the new flux of people. A local townsman named VM Slipher spearheaded a campaign to raise money to build a more modern hotel in a new location. His efforts produced a municipal bond that would fund the new hotel. In 1926, funds and investments totaling $200,000 were raised from prominent residents of Flagstaff including the writer Zane Grey. By June of the same year the ground was broken for Hotel Monte Vista.

Originally called Community Hotel, the 73-room hotel opened New Years Day 1927. Later, through a contest, the name was changed to Hotel Monte Vista.

Though the hotel opened during prohibition, the location housed a profitable bootlegging operation and speakeasy. In 1931, police raided the establishment and closed it down, but two years later prohibition was lifted and the hotel reopened.

During the 1940s and 1950s, many movie stars stayed at Hotel Monte Vista due to its first class accommodations. Some of the celebrities included Jane Russell, Gary Cooper, Bing Crosby, John Wayne, and local favorite Zane Grey.

The hotel was publicly owned until the 1960s and then sold to a private owner. Today it is on the National Register of Historic Places.

The Ghosts...

Ghost stories about the Hotel Monte Vista have been circulating since the 1950s. In the lobby, furniture has been known to move, the telephone rings by itself, and objects are removed and then found later in the same place. Employees have reported Big Band music playing when there is no band.

One of the first specter sightings reported was from John Wayne, who had stayed in Room 210, now called the Zane Grey Room. Wayne explained that he saw the apparition of a bellboy come into his room. The apparition seemed benevolent and he didn't feel threatening

Throughout the years, many have reported a similar ghost story. Some have been awakened in the middle of the night by a knock on the door and a voice stating, "Room Service"...only when they go to the door no one is there. Others have witnessed an apparition of a bellboy standing at the door of the Zane Grey Room and then disappear before their eyes. Some have seen the specter of a white woman wandering down the hall near the room.

The Scarlet Women

The Red Light District was situated two blocks from Hotel Monte Vista just over the railroad tracks. In the 1940s, two "scarlet women" used Room 306 to conduct their "business." Both were murdered and thrown out the third-floor window into the street. Now, guests experience being woken by a presence standing over their bed or a feeling of being watched.

Male guests explain they have had the sensation of being choked in their sleep, or the hands of a female covering their nose and mouth. After being awakened, they could not fall asleep due to a feeling of anxiousness or impending doom.

One Last Drink

Some ghost stories are unusual as much as they are intriguing. Human nature can seem odd sometimes, especially when confronted with the face of death. In the 1970s, three men robbed a bank near Hotel Monte Vista. The trio nearly escaped the police, but one man was shot. Ignoring the wound, the injured man and his two friends decided to get a drink in the hotel lounge to celebrate their victory. While drinking his last drink, the bank robber bled to death and fell to the floor.

Now, patrons have reported an eerie presence watching them as they have a drink at the bar. Staff has witnessed glasses and bar stools moving on their own accord while some have heard a disembodied voice say, "Good Morning," as they walk into the lounge.

The Meat Chandelier

In the 1980s, a long-term boarder in Room 220 had an eccentric habit of hanging raw meat from the room chandelier. He died in the room and his body was not found until three days later.

When the room was being renovated, a repairman went to get some materials. He turned off the lights, locked the door, and left. A few minutes later, when he came back, the TV was turned on full blast, the lights were on, and the linens were ripped off the bed and strewn around the room.

The Rocking Woman

Room 305 is perhaps the most active room in the hotel. The phenomena seem to be nearly always present. The source of it is said to be an older woman who was a long-time tenant in the room. Often, she sat in her favorite rocking chair staring out the window. Nobody knew if she was waiting for someone or just enjoyed the view. Eventually, the woman died in the room.

Now, many have witnessed a phantom woman rocking in a chair by the window. Sometimes the rocking chair moves by itself.

The Crying Baby

The basement holds the most intriguing and disturbing paranormal activity. Housekeeping staff and laundry personnel have reported hearing an infant crying. Nobody has found the source, but the crying is said to become so loud that staff will run up the stairs to get away from it.

Section Six:

The Superstition Mountains

Directions: From Interstate 8 East, exit at Dunaway Road and go north. Turn east onto County Highway S80 (Evan Hewes Highway). Turn north onto Huff Road. Turn west onto Wheeler Road and follow to the base of the mountain.

THE HISTORY

Though situated just outside Central Arizona, the mysterious deaths and intrigue surrounding the Superstition Mountains are well worth the short trip for the paranormal aficionado. Perhaps you will meet one of the many lost souls whose life was ended prematurely, wandering around the ragged cliffs and peaks. Perhaps they will tell you their tale, or maybe you will be granted access to the lost mine by the Thunder God. Better still...you may even live to tell about it.

The Superstition Mountains are located just outside of Phoenix near Apache Junction on Route 60. Its rugged terrain is comprised of jagged cliffs, plateaus, and mesas that make it difficult to hike. Much of the mountain range has not been explored. The craggy peaks and jagged rocks are considered so extreme that NASA used the mountain range to train astronauts for the terrain in space. Some Apaches believe that the entrance to the underworld resides in the mountains, and wind blowing from the opening cause dust storms in the area. Hundreds of people have died in the mountains. Many have hiked through its rough terrain...never to be seen again. Others were ruthlessly murdered. Most of these deaths were shrouded in supernatural intrigue and the greedy pursuit of gold.

Like most areas in Arizona, the Apache Indians first inhabited the Superstition Mountains. In the 1500s, Spanish conquistadors traveled through the area searching for gold. Francisco Vasquez de Coronado and his band of men traveled north from Mexico in search of "The Seven Golden Cities of Cibola," which were legendary cities filled with gold and other treasures. When Coronado reached the area that would become Superstition Mountain, the Apache Indians told him there was gold in the mountains. When he asked to be led to the riches, the Apaches refused in fear of angering the Thunder God that lived in the mountain range. Coronado was warned if anyone were to trespass on the sacred ground of the Thunder God they would surely be destroyed.

Ignoring the warning, Coronado sent his group into the mountains to search for the gold, but as the men hiked the mountain...they would *disappear* one by one. It is said that if a man strayed from his companion he would never be seen again. Later the bodies were found mutilated and their heads severed. Many of the survivors refused to ever set foot on the mountain again, fearing for their own mortality. Coronado called the rugged terrain Monte Superstition because of the mysterious way his men died. Regarded as evil, many other Spaniards were told the horrific tale of Coronado's men and stayed away from the mountain range, but the lure of gold would attract others in the coming years — and that would, inevitably, seal their demise.

In 1845, Don Miguel Peralta was the first person to find a vein of gold in Superstition Mountain, using the directions from the horrific tales of the Coronado party. Peralta was a Spaniard and a prominent member of the community who owned a ranch near Sonora, Mexico. Before traveling back to his homeland for an excavation party and supplies, he memorized the land, searching for a detailed landmark. Peralta decided that the most prominent point of Superstition Mountain looked like a sombrero, so he titled his findings, "The Sombrero Mines."

To the Indians, the point was thought to be the finger of the Thunder God, and they aptly named the landmark, "The Finger of God." Later, Anglo prospectors would search the area for gold, particularly Pauline Weaver, who etched his name into the landmark's rock. Other prospectors saw the etching and called the point, "Weavers Needle," and the nickname stuck.

Peralta traveled back home to Mexico and returned to Superstition Mine with an excavation crew including burros and wagons. From memory, he found the mine, and soon was sending millions of pesos worth of gold back to Mexico. In 1848, the Apaches were not happy with the presence of Peralta's crew in their sacred mountains and vowed to stop him. Peralta was warned of the impending fight between his crew and the Indians. Afraid, he decided to pack up his party and whatever gold they had procured to go home. Peralta took great precautions to hide the mouth of his mine, wiping out any trace of its existence, so that no one would find it, just in case he decided to come back at a later date. Unfortunately, this would be last time Peralta set foot on Superstition Mountain.

At dawn, he and his crew were to head back to Mexico, but they never had the chance. Apache Indians ambushed the band of Spaniards, slaying each and every one. Panicked, the pack mules (carrying the leather bags of gold) scattered, falling off cliffs to their death. For years after the incident, other prospectors and soldiers stumbled upon the dead carcasses of burros and old leather bags filled with gold. Eventually, the strip of land called, "The Gold Field," became well-known to bandits and others who were looking to get rich quick by scavenging through the remains of the Peralta party. The last known man to find riches in the area was in 1914. C. H. Silverlocks traveled to Phoenix showing off his booty: leather from a deteriorated bag, a few pieces of Spanish silver, and $18,000 in gold.

But more stories lie in wait...

The Tales...

The Good Doctor

Only one person was able to reap the benefits of Superstition Mountain and live to tell about it. His name was Dr. Abraham Thorne. He was born in East Saint Louis, Illinois, but his whole life he dreamed of heading west to become a doctor to the Indians. Thorne was befriended by Kit Carson, a fur trapper who would later become an integral part in Indian negotiations during the Civil War.

Due to his trapper expertise, Carson was employed as the hunter for the garrison of Bent's Fort. Through his connections, when Fort McDowell became a territory in 1865, Carson arranged for Thorne to become an army doctor with an officer's rank.

Rivalry between the Indians and the white settlers was fierce and often times extreme. Many fights broke out between the pioneers and Apache, both sides losing countless casualties. In an effort to create a truce between the opposing forces, President Abraham Lincoln proposed a neutral territory for the Apache located along the Verde River near Fort McDowell. Thorne came to work in the area, nicknamed "The Strip" by the white settlers and soldiers. There he worked for the Indians, caring for their elderly and sick, delivering babies, and teaching hygiene. Soon, Carson earned the respect of the tribal leaders and he became an ally to the Apache.

In 1870, Thorne was taken aside by the elders of the tribe to be offered a unique proposal. They deemed him a worthy man and in return for his good deeds to the tribe, the Indians would take him to a place where he could find gold. The catch was he had to be blindfolded for the entire twenty-mile journey.

Trusting the Apache, Thorne agreed to the terms. A blindfold was placed over his eyes and a bag over his head during the travel on horseback. When the cloth was finally removed from his eyes, he found himself in an unknown canyon. Later, he would write that he saw a pointed pinnacle of rock about a mile south from where he was situated. Most believe the landmark Thorne referred to was Weavers Needle. He was not near anything that resembled a mine. However, in front of him laid a huge pile of gold. Thorne took the gold and sold it for $6,000.

The Lost Dutchman

The story of the Lost Dutchman, Jacob Walz (or Waltz depending on the resource), is the backbone of the myths surrounding Superstition Mountain. Ironically, Walz was not Dutch; he was German. However, at the time, it was customary to call German immigrants "Dutchman" as an inaccurate offshoot of the word "Duetsch" meaning German.

In 1810, Walz was born in Oberschwandorf, Wuttenburg, Germany. He immigrated to New York some time in 1835 and then traveled to North Carolina after hearing stories about men striking it rich in the goldfields. His first attempt at finding a vein of gold failed, so he traveled to Georgia and Mississippi in search of ever-elusive riches.

Like many other immigrants searching for ore, Walz was misinformed about the law concerning mining. In Mississippi, he realized he had to become a United States citizen first before staking a mining claim. So, even if he had struck it rich in the goldfields, he would not have been able to keep it. In 1848, Walz filed a letter of intent to become a United States citizen.

Having no luck in Mississippi, in 1850, Walz packed his bags and set out to travel west to the California goldfields. He worked as a prospector and miner for ten years in the Sierra Nevada hills; though never finding the "mother lode," he procured enough gold to keep himself motivated. In 1861, Walz finally became a naturalized citizen of the United States of America. For awhile, he worked as a miner on the San Gabriel River near Follower's Camp with a man name Ruben Blakney.

This is where he met Elisha M. Reavis, a former teacher turned gold prospector who had a claim about 1,500 yards from the Blakney Camp. Later Reavis would be known as the Hermit of Superstition Mountain.

In 1863, Walz left California with the Peeple-Weaver party headed for the Bradshaw Mountains in the Arizona territory. He was well into his fifties by 1868 and questioning whether or not he would ever find his "mother lode." The Indians nicknamed him "Snowbeard" because of his long white beard. That same year he started to settle down putting a homestead claim on 160 acres of land on the north bank of the Salt River near the Superstition Mountain range. As soon as Walz arrived, he started to hear stories about the region: stories of the Apaches and their Thunder God and stories about large deposits of gold in the mountains.

It's not clear what happened next in the story of the Lost Dutchman mythology. There are conflicting stories about how Walz acquired his fortune, but all agree that he somehow came into a large sum of gold that was unaccounted for. According to documents, Walz staked claims in the Prescott area and never mined near Superstition Mountain. Some believe all the years of mining finally paid off and he struck it rich in Prescott even though there aren't any corresponding documents to support that his claims were ever prosperous. Others believe an entirely different tale.

It is known that when Walz moved to the Arizona territory, he consulted for the Vulture Gold Mine owned by Henry Wickenburg. It is said he met an Apache woman name Ken-tee who was a worker in the mine. Eventually Ken-tee became his mistress and the two lived together in the camps. The pair was suspected of high-grading ore (stealing choice pieces of gold ore) and an inquiry was held. As part of the inquiry, their living quarters were searched, but the ore was never found. Still, Walz and Ken-tee were dismissed from Vulture Mine. Some believe the stolen gold was hidden in another location and later the old prospector picked it up. Others speculate this was only the beginning of the story and the riches Walz would collect.

It is suggested that during her love affair with Walz, the Apache woman told him the exact location of the gold in Superstition Mountain, even taking him to the mine. When Ken-tee arrived from Phoenix with Walz and $70,000 of ore, her relatives were sure she had spilled the secret location of the mines. Within seventy-two hours, the Apaches attacked Walz and Ken-tee at his Salt River home — a battle that lasted two days. Walz managed to escape with only a shoulder wound from being stuck by an arrow. Ken-tee was captured and her tongue was sliced out of her mouth. Neighbors retrieved her, but the wound was too deep and she bled to death within an hour of her rescue.

Saddened and embittered, Walz retreated to Phoenix and went into seclusion. It is said he built a saloon in the Tortilla Flats and spent a great deal of his time drinking and starting brawls. Time went by and he was almost forgotten. Then one day he showed up in a Phoenix bar buying drinks with gold nuggets, only to disappear for months and then reappear with more gold.

Many assumed he was traveling back and forth to a hidden mining location. They were curious of the location because his leather bag was always full of the purest gold anyone had laid their eyes on. Curious prospectors asked the old miner where his mine was located, but his directions were always vague or contradictory. On a few occasions he was followed by curious get-rich-schemers, but he always lost his pursuers in the rugged terrain near Superstition Mountain.

The Two Jacobs

It is unclear who Jacob Weiser was or how he came to be part of the Lost Dutchman mythology. It is thought that Walz met Weiser at the Vulture Gold Mines and the two instantly became friends because of their similar German heritage. Weiser was thought to be the invisible partner in the Vulture Gold Mines high-grading scheme, taking the gold to an undisclosed location and meeting up with Walz and Ken-tee later. Some suggest he was also there for the Apache siege where Ken-tee lost her life, but she was killed for no reason because she had not disclosed the whereabouts of the mine in Superstition Mountain.

Instead, one story says that Walz and Weiser were tenacious, experienced miners who were staking claim in the Superstition Mountains and accidentally found a pure vein of gold. Others tell a more gruesome tale where the German miners stumbled upon two men who were mistaken for Indians and shot down. Only later did the prospectors realize the men were Mexicans who were mining gold.

But the most accepted story states that Walz and Weiser were given a map by a Mexican man they saved in a knife fight. The man was Don Miguel Peralta, the descendent of the original Peralta party that were brutally murdered by the Apache so many years before. As a reward for saving Peralta, the German miners were allowed to take a look at the family map that showed the specific location of the mine. Peralta suggested the three men travel to the mine and split the shares three ways. Walz and Weiser agreed, and the trio set off to Superstition Mountain to stake their claim. With the directions of the map, the mine was easy to find. However, they did not account for the watchful eye of the Apache Indians. They were attacked by a war party, but managed to narrowly escape with $60,000 of gold, which they sold in nearby Tucson.

Fearing he would encounter the same fate as his relative, Peralta vowed never to return to the mountain range and sold the map to Walz and Weiser for their share of the profits. The two Jacobs went back to the mine for a total of two years. They were a good team and devised a system to keep the Apache from attacking. One would stand outside with a shotgun and the other would fill sacks with ore. But soon their good luck would change to the supernatural fate of Superstition Mountain.

One night, a supply mule got loose and pulled their food provisions from a tree where it was being stored, leaving them with very little supplies. Walz went into town to replace their food while Weiser stayed at the camp. The old miner was gone for five days, and when he rode up to the camp, he found that Apaches had raided it. All the animals were missing and Weiser was found spread-eagle over a campfire, burned to death. Walz was so shocked by the state of his camp, he traveled to Phoenix without food or water. The town's folk found him in a bar ravished from hunger, ranting about the Apache attack. Later, when Walz had calmed down, he went back to retrieve Weiser's belongings and buried his body near the mine. When he came back to Phoenix, Walz was accused of killing Weiser to claim his portion of the profits. Walz dared the prospectors to go to Superstition Mountain and find the unmarked grave near the mine.

From the point of Weiser's demise, the story stays the same. Walz became a recluse, periodically showing up in bars with leather bags of pure gold. Only instead of mining it from Superstition Mountain, it is thought that Walz and Weiser stockpiled their two years worth of ore in an unknown hiding spot near their campsite. The old miner would take trips to the secret hiding place when he needed money. He would tie blankets to the back of his horse to brush away the tracks.

The Baker and the Brothers

By 1890, Jacob Walz was eighty-years-old and had trouble keeping secret the location of the mine because he was not physically able to fend off interlopers anymore. He decided it was time to hole up the mine indefinitely. Walz went to great lengths to conceal the mine by holing it up with timber in a crisscross pattern, filling it up with dirt, and placing rocks from the area over the dirt so it matched the terrain.

Walz kept up his reclusive lifestyle, retiring at his Salt River home for the rest of his days. He befriended a mulatto woman from Louisiana named Julia Thomas who owned a bakery in Phoenix. He sold the woman eggs she used for her baked goods.

In February, torrential rains poured down in the Phoenix area, flooding the lands. Walz ran outside to coop up his chickens and other livestock to keep them safe. The water levels rose higher, trapping the old miner outside. He climbed a tree to keep from drowning, and got stuck there for two days and two nights with only his head and shoulders out of the water.

After the rains subsided, at the request of Thomas, Herman and Reinhardt Petrasch went in search of Walz to make sure he had survived the flood. They found him on his bed, shivering violently from wet and cold. He conveyed the story of his time trapped on the tree and said that when the rains had finally stopped he was able to make it to his home. The Petraschs put a sick Walz on their horse and took him to see Thomas, where she was housing flood victims.

Walz became seriously ill due to his long stay in the icy waters of the flood. In a feverish state, he proclaimed that he had forgotten something of value at the house. He asked the Petraschs if they would go to his house and find the thing of value. The men kept explaining to the old man that his house had been severely damaged by the water, leaving only the foundation. Walz kept insisting they go back, and finally the men relented. The Petraschs went back to the wreckage of the home. They searched the rubble and found three bags full of gold worth $15,000. The Petraschs took the gold back to the old man and put it in a candle box under his bed.

Health-wise, Waltz never recovered from the flood and he contracted pneumonia. Thomas tried to nurse the old miner back to good health. The pair became close during his convalescence and he spoke candidly about the mine in Superstition Mountain. Walz promised Thomas, as gratitude for her kindness, that he would take her to the mine in the spring. Unfortunately, Walz would not live to see the spring, dying in October 1891. However, before his death, to keep true to his word, he tried to explain to Thomas the whereabouts of the mine so that she could make a map. Walz had suffered a series of strokes that left him partially paralyzed. It was hard for him to speak and he was never quite able to give a true recollection of the mine's location.

Shortly after the death of Jacob Walz, Julia Thomas financed an expedition with the Petrasch brothers to search for the lost mine in the Superstition Mountains. Anxious to find gold, the party decided to take their excursion in the blazing heat of midsummer. They stayed in the mountains nearly five weeks searching for the mines with the context clues given by Walz on his deathbed. Unfortunately, Thomas and the Petrasch brothers came back from Superstition Mountain empty-handed and disappointed.

To recoup some of her losses, Thomas designed a map from the information she learned from Walz and sold it to eager prospectors. The Petrasch brothers and their father continued to search the Superstition Mountains for the Lost Dutchman Mine nearly their whole lives. After a few futile excursions together, Rhinehart accused his brother, Herman, of not understanding the descriptions of the mine that Walz confessed on his deathbed. The two argued and never spoke to each other again. Both brothers searched for the mine independently. Later in life, Rhinehart's eyesight began to fail. Disappointed and embittered, he realized he would never find the mine and shot himself in the head. Herman died shortly after of natural causes.

The Madman of Superstition Mountain

Originally from Beardstown, Illinois, Elisha M. Reavis was a well-educated teacher who would later become one of the many casualties of Superstition Mountain. Disinterested in teaching, Reavis packed up his bags and headed west to California, where he staked a claim along the San Gabriel River. He had very little luck in the area and, with other miners, traveled to the Bradshaw Mountains in the Arizona Territory. Reavis never struck it rich; by the 1870s, he had settled down on a small piece of land near Superstition Mountain, selling vegetables to other prospectors and townspeople.

Reavis was notorious for eccentric, reclusive behavior; he never cut his hair, shaved, or bathed. Many times he was spotted running naked through the rugged trails of the mountain range with a shotgun aimed high in the air. Other times, he would spend weeks in his small farmhouse, reading books and keeping to himself. His behavior was erratic and unpredictable. For this he was nicknamed the "The Madman of Superstition Mountain" or "The Hermit of Superstition Mountain."

Reavis was an extremely accurate marksman with a shotgun and gained a reputation for shooting down attacking Apache warriors from long distances. He was not a man to be reckoned with and was left to his own devices, even by the Indians.

Though Reavis was known for disappearing for weeks at a time, eventually he would show up at the mining camps to sell vegetables. When he was not seen for some time, his friends went to check on him. Reavis was not at his cabin and a search party was put together to search for the old man. Four miles south of his home he was found dead, his body severed from his head, which was found a few feet away. Did the Apache finally have their way with him? Did he fall prey to the curse of Superstition Mountain? Nobody knows for sure what happened to "The Hermit," but he is only one of many who lost their heads...

Other Victims of the Mountains

Throughout the years, many heeded the call of the Superstition Mountains...only to fall victim of an untimely death. They include:

☠ In 1880, two soldiers recently discharged from Fort Mc Dowell arrived in Pinal looking for work at the King Silver Mine. They showed a bag of rich gold ore to mine operator Aaron Mason, asking him to assess it for them. The two soldiers said they found the gold while crossing through the Superstition Mountain range. Mason asked the soldiers if they could retrace their footsteps and relocate the spot where they found the gold. They explained that the mine was in a northern direction near a sharp pinnacle (which Mason thought to be Weaver's Needle) in extremely rugged country. A narrow path led into a valley and straight to the mine.

Mason convinced the soldiers to go back to Superstition Mountain to find the mine. He bought their gold for $700 and outfitted them for a mining excursion. The two left the next day and never returned. Mason waited two weeks before summoning a search party to look for the soldiers. They found the first man naked and shot in the head at the base of a path leading to the mountain. The second man was found the next day farther down the trail in the same condition.

☠ Joe Dearing, a prospector and part-time bartender, heard the stories of the dead soldiers circulating through Pinal. Intrigued by the lost mine, he decided to take a trip to Superstition Mountain and see if he could find the location himself. Dearing came back from his excursion pleased that he had found the location of the mine. He said the mine was pit shaped like a funnel with a large opening at the top. The pit had been partially filled with debris and a tunnel had been walled-in by rocks. Dearing got a job at the King Silver Mine to save up enough money to put together an excavating party that would take him to Superstition Mountain. Unfortunately, a cave-in at the mine killed him exactly one week later.

Two prospectors known as Malm and Silverlock excavated at the northern base of Superstition Mountain. They found some dispersed gold from the Peralta massacre but little else. Still the pair stayed in the area for over a year mining for gold. Then one day Malm stalked into the Mormon cooperative ranting and raving incoherently. He accused Silverlock of trying to kill him. The local deputies took him in and he was deemed insane and committed to the local territorial asylum.

In 1910, the skeleton of a young woman was found in a cave high in Superstition Mountain. A few gold nuggets were placed next to the body. A coroner determined the body was recent. No other information was ever brought forth about the woman or how she got the gold.

In 1927, there were two incidents with boulders. A man from New Jersey and his son were hiking in the area, when an unknown person began rolling boulders over the cliffs above. A large rock hit the boy crushing his legs. Later the same year, deer hunters in the area were chased off by someone attempting to drop boulders on them.

Adolph Ruth, a government employee from Washington D.C., headed into the Superstition Mountain foothills in June 1931. With an old Peralta map, he set out to find the Lost Dutchman mine...and was never seen again. A search party was sent to find him. They found his camp, but not his body. In December, his skull was found on Black Top Mountain with two holes in it. A month later, his skeleton was discovered about a mile away from his head. Tacked to his body was a note that stated, "About 200 feet across from the cave." The map was nowhere to be found.

In 1937, prospector Guy "Hematite" Frink found gold in the mountains. That November he was found on the side of a trail with a bullet hole in his stomach and a bag of gold at his side.

☠ In 1947, an innovative prospector named James A. Cravey flew into the Superstition Mountains by helicopter. He was dropped down near Weavers Needle...never to be seen again. A search party found his camp, but he was nowhere to be found. Months later, his headless skeleton was found wrapped in a blanket. Later, his head was found thirty feet away.

The stories are endless as the years go on. From prospectors to family outings, there are dozens more tales of missing persons and "accidental" deaths. Does the Apache Thunder God live in the mountains? Does he protect the sacred land by smiting greedy miners? Is the land cursed by all the spilled blood upon its rocks? Is there really a "lost" mine with veins of pure gold ore lining its walls? Did old man Walz locate the mine with his friend Weiser?

One thing is for sure: whether it's supernatural or not, there have been an unusual amount of deaths in one small area of land. You can hike parts of Superstition Mountain by visiting the Lost Dutchman Park. Mining is no longer allowed on the mountain range due to the large number of casualties. However, it is assured that there are spirits of unrest lurking through its peaks and valleys, longing to tell their tale to anyone who will listen. Perhaps, if you walk down the same paths as those who came before you and lost their lives, you will hear their call luring you into the mountains. They will tell you the secrets of Superstition Mountain, and hopefully you will come out alive.

GLOSSARY

Glossary

After Life: A generic term for existence after death, particularly in the world of spirits.

Altered States of Consciousness (ASC): Any mental state that is not the normal waking. Altered states of consciousness include dreaming, hypnosis, trance, and meditation.

Anomaly: An unconventional phenomenon that cannot be explained by conventional science. Sometimes referred to as "paranormal."

Amulet: An object that is thought to bring protection from spirits or evil to the wearer.

Apparition: A ghost or an impression of a person or animal (sometimes inanimate objects) that is experienced by sight or extra sensory perception.

Astral Body: An exact replica of the corporeal body, which can leave the physical body temporarily for astral traveling or an out-of-body-experience. During death the astral body leaves permanently. Sometimes referred to as an "etheric body."

Aura: Latin for "breath of air," it's a radiating halo of multi-colored vibrations surrounding the living body.

Automatic: Writing an automatic motor response in which a person's hand writes significant sentences or phrases without the writer's premeditated conscious awareness.

Channeling: Receiving information directly from a consciousness (dead or alive) or a nonphysical entity, usually through trance or automatic writing.

Clairaudience: The ability to hear sounds through other means than the physical auditory system.

Clairsentience: The ability to sense what others cannot with the five human senses.

Clairvoyance (Mind over Distance): The ability to gain information about an object, location, or physical event through means other than the known human senses. Sometimes called remote viewing.

Cold Reading: Information said to be received by paranormal means, but in fact are generalizations based on facial expressions and context clues in conversation.

Crisis Apparition: The presence of a person close to death who projects an image of himself to a loved one or an acquaintance near their time of death.

Crystalmancy: A technique of gazing into a crystal ball, a clear pool of water or any clear surface.

Déjà vu: French for "already seen," it's the feeling of having experienced a place or event even though it has usually not occurred the first time. Sometimes referred to as "false memory," or "memory without recognition. If déjà vu coincides with clairvoyance, then it is called "promnesia."

Direct Voice Phenomenon (DVP): A spirit voice that is spoken directly to the participants of a séance.

Divination: Receiving paranormal information through tools such as tarot cards, dowsing rods, and tea leaves.

Dowsing: Using dowsing rods to locate water or paranormal energy.

Ectoplasm: An exterior substance produced from the body of a physical medium.

Electromagnetic Field (EMF): A physical influence that arises from electrically charged objects that permeates through all of space. Electromagnetism is one of the four fundamental forces of nature.

Electronic Voice Phenomenon (EVP): Voices or sounds heard on recorded audio through playback that was not present during the time of the recording.

Extrasensory Perception (ESP): Obtaining information through means other than the normal senses. Extrasensory perception encompasses phenomenon such as telepathy, clairvoyance, precognition, and presentiment.

Ghost: An apparition or entity of a deceased person or animal.

Haunting: Recurring paranormal phenomena in a location that includes apparitions, disembodied voices, and moving objects.

Intuition: Coming to an idea or conclusion without reasoning and intellect and from a source that is outside the consciousness. Usually the source is thought to be paranormal or mystical.

Lucid Dream: A dream where the dreamer has an awareness that he is dreaming.

Meditation: A general term for achieving an altered state of consciousness by stilling the mind to recognize more subtle perceptions for self-awareness.

Medium: A person who can regularly contact the spirit world at will.

Near Death Experience (NDE): An experience reported by those who nearly died. Usually the person reports core experiences that include feelings of peace, an out-of-body experience, viewing a bright light, or being greeted by deceased relatives.

Occult: Latin for "covered or concealed," it's a group whose practices include esoteric knowledge such as magic, astrology, and witchcraft.

Out-of-Body-Experience (OBE): An experience in which one feels they are entirely bodiless or tied to their body by a silver cord. They usually view their own inert bodies and can perceive events happening around them.

Paranormal: Any phenomenon that exceeds the limits of what is deemed physically possible.

Parapsychology: The scientific study of three kinds of unusual events associated with human experience: ESP, mind-matter interaction, and phenomena suggestive of survival after death, including near-death experiences, apparitions, and reincarnation.

Past-Life Regression: A process in which a person is hypnotized and regressed to experience a past life, suggesting the idea of reincarnation.

Place Memory: The ability of a location to hold impressions of people and events that transpired there.

Poltergeist: German for "noisy ghost," a psychokinesis phenomenon is often attributed to a mischievous spirit. It's thought to be due to a living person or group of people. Although reported in all age groups, the agent is most frequently an adolescent.

Precognition: To perceive information about places or events before they happen either in waking consciousness or in a dream state. Also referred to as a premonition.

Presentiment (Mind over Time): Receiving information about future events that is perceived as emotions. Unconsciously, the person knew what was coming before it occurred.

Psi: A general term for para-psychological phenomena. Psi, psychic, and psychical are synonyms.

Psychokinesis (PK): Direct mental interaction with physical objects, animate or inanimate; the direct influence of mind on a physical system that cannot be accounted for by any known physical energy. Examples include distorting or moving an object, or influencing the output of a random number generator.

Psychometry: Also referred to as telekinesis, Psychometry is receiving information by making physical contact with an object. Sometimes referred to as "token object reading."

Reincarnation: The belief that the soul or aspects of self are reborn into another body and repeated throughout many lives.

Remote Viewing: A general term for extrasensory perception, especially when in context of describing a geographical location.

Retrocognition: Receiving information from the past by extrasensory perception or other paranormal means.

Scrying: A technique for acquiring paranormal impressions in the form of pictures or hallucinations by staring into a black mirror, fire, tea leaves, or a crystal ball.

Séance: French for "to sit," it's a meeting of one or more persons, usually hosted by a medium, with the intent of communicating with the deceased or to experience paranormal phenomenon.

Spiritualism: A movement based around the belief of life after death and the practice of spirit communication usually via medium.

Survival: Continued existence of the consciousness after death.

Table Tilting: A motor response in which several persons put their fingertips on a table causing it to move in a series of taps or raps. The messages are assumed to be communication from the deceased. Also referred to as "table tipping" or "table turning."

Telepathy (Direct Mind-to-Mind Communication): The transfer of thoughts or feelings between individuals by means other then the five senses.

Zener Cards: The original name for ESP cards (circle, cross, square, star, and wavy lines). The cards are named after psychologist Karl Zener, who suggested the shapes be used on the cards.

Contributors

RUDY CORTESE

Rudy Cortese is a full time musician playing concerts, festivals, corporate/private functions, and a variety of other venues throughout the United States. He has played banjo and guitar for over twenty years. He is the current reigning Arizona State Banjo Champion and two-time winner of the Four Corner State Banjo Championship.

Rudy has taught banjo, guitar, mandolin, and vocals for students in the Tucson/Phoenix, Arizona area. He also is a serious songwriter and composer for the banjo and bluegrass music. He is currently playing with "Cadillac Mountain," a popular local Tucson fixture in the music community, and with the bluegrass group Whistle Stop throughout Arizona, California, and Colorado. For more information about Whistle Stop, visit their website at www.myspace.com/whistlestopbluegrass.

Rudy has opened for James King, Cherryholmes Family, Allen Mills, Jim and Jesse McReynolds, Jerry Douglas, and many other popular bluegrass artists. He has played with the band Crucial County and, at the 2001 Huck Finn Jubilee Festival, the band was awarded third runner up in the countrywide competition. This festival was also awarded the Bluegrass Event of the Year at the 2001 IBMA Awards.

Rudy is currently playing with the bluegrass group Whistle Stop throughout Arizona, California, and Colorado. For more information about Whistle Stop, visit their website at www.myspace.com/whistlestopbluegrass.

Rudy is also is currently writing a series of children's books based on bluegrass music. Accompanying these stories will be original compositions and recordings involving each instrument of the bluegrass genre.

Gail Cortese

Gail Cortese is currently a Registered Nurse working via telephone with patients who have chronic conditions. She has been in the medical related field for more than thirty; she spent twenty years in insurance and then at the age of 48 returned to school and obtained her RN degree, and subsequent to that, has obtained her Bachelors in Science Management.

Gail is a mother of two adult sons, grandmother to three, and currently resides in Gilbert, Arizona.

STACY FORTSON

Stacy has worked for a credit union for over seven years as an accountant. She has a bachelor's degree in Accounting and is currently working towards her master's in Business Administration. Stacy enjoys scuba diving, photography, and paranormal investigation.

Stacy has been interested in paranormal activity since a young age and has been a paranormal investigator since August 2008. She's been lucky enough to experience the unknown on many occasions. She says that the opportunity to work with P.I.S.A. Paranormal has been an experience that is "beyond words and all positive." Her goal is to learn and help others cope with paranormal activity.

BIBLIOGRAPHY

Bibliography

Books

Branning, Debe. *Sleeping with Ghosts! A Ghost Hunter's Guide to Arizona's Haunted Hotels and Inns*. Phoenix, Arizona: Golden West Publishers, Inc., 2007

Dongo, Tom. *Everything You Wanted to Know About Sedona in a Nutshell*. Self-Published.

Robson, Ellen. *Haunted Arizona: Ghosts of the Grand Canyon State*. Phoenix, Arizona: Gold West Publishers, Inc., 2003

Websites

http://en.wikipedia.org/wiki/Ann_Miller

http://en.wikipedia.org/wiki/Kit_Carson

http://en.wikipedia.org/wiki/Mae_West

http://en.wikipedia.org/wiki/Maynard_James_Keenan
http://en.wikipedia.org/wiki/Zane_Grey

http://www.aaevp.com/articles/articles_about_evp11.html

http://www.aipl.org/aj/superstition/stories/Elisha%20M%20Reavis.pdf

http://www.arizona-leisure.com/arizona-haunted-hotels.html

http://www.assap.org/newsite/articles/Thermal%20imaging%20ghosts.html

http://www.assap.org/newsite/htmlfiles/Glossary.html

http://www.azjerome.com/pages/cottonwood/cottonwood.html

http://www.connorhotel.com/history.html

http://www.desertusa.com/Cities/az/flagstaff.html

http://www.enotes.com/history-fact-finder/exploration-settlement/what-were-seven-cities-cibola

http://www.epinions.com/content_102009048708

http://www.fabuloustravel.com/usa/articles/393/21969

http://www.flagstaffarizona.org/downloads/visitors/flagstaff_history.pdf

http://www.geocities.com/dustinmdudley/arizona_jerome.html

http://www.ghostfirehaunts.com/emf.html

http://www.ghosthauntings.suite101.com/article.cfm/ghost_hunting_equipment_emf_meter

http://www.ghost-tech.com/franks.php

http://www.goldenstateparanormal.com/glossary.html

http://www.hauntedamericatours.com/ghosthunting/Ovilus.php

http://www.hauntedhouses.com/states/az/jerome_grand_hotel.cfm

http://www.home.comcast.net/~parainvestigator/articles/Ions.html

http://www.hotelmontevista.com/

http://www.jeromegrandhotel.net/Jerome_History.html

http://www.legendsofamerica.com/AZ-Monte-Vista.html

http://www.lovessedona.com/01.html

http://www.museumoftalkingboards.com/history.html

http://www.my-arizona-desert-living.com/Lost-Dutchman-Mine.html

http://www.mysticalblaze.com/GlossaryParanormal.html

http://www.parapsych.org/historical_terms.html

http://www.prairieghosts.com/conspirit.html

http://www.prairieghosts.com/dowsing.html

http://www.prairieghosts.com/dutchman.html

http://www.prairieghosts.com/jerome.html

http://www.prairieghosts.com/polter.html

Bibliography

http://www.prairieghosts.com/resid.html

http://www.prairieghosts.com/sedona.html

http://www.jeff.scott.tripod.com/flagstaff.html

http://www.sedonaaz.gov/sedona/history.aspx

http://www.sedonadrivetours.com/3-chapel.html

http://www.sgha.net/az/jerome/innatjerome.html

http://www.spiritroom.com/history.html

http://www.superstitionmountainmuseum.org/LostDutchmanExhibit.html

http://www.theoutlaws.com/gold.html

http://www.vacationideas.me/usa/jerome-arizona-grand-hotel-america-most-haunted/

http://www.virtualology.com/kit-carson.com

http://www.visionsofheaven.com/journeys-sedonadocs/sedBell.html

http://www.weatherfordhotel.com/history_early.html

http://www.yourghoststories.com/glossary.php

Index

Index

Index

Index